Maryln Appelbaum

How to
Handle

HARD-TO-HANDLE

PARENTS

A JOINT PUBLICATION

CORWIN
A SAGE Company

ATi

For information:

Corwin
A SAGE Company
2455 Teller Road
Thousand Oaks, California 91320
(800) 233-9936
Fax: (800) 417-2466
www.corwinpress.com

SAGE Ltd.
1 Oliver's Yard
55 City Road
London EC1Y 1SP
United Kingdom

SAGE India Pvt. Ltd.
B 1/I 1 Mohan Cooperative
   Industrial Area
Mathura Road, New Delhi 110 044
India

SAGE Asia-Pacific Pte. Ltd.
33 Pekin Street #02-01
Far East Square
Singapore 048763

Printed in the United States of America

Library of Congress Cataloging-in-Publication Data

Appelbaum, Maryln.
How to handle hard-to-handle parents / Maryln Appelbaum.
        p. cm.
"A Joint Publication with the Appelbaum Training Institute."
Includes bibliographical references and index.
ISBN 978-1-4129-6440-1 (cloth)
ISBN 978-1-4129-6441-8 (pbk.)

   1. Parent-teacher relationships—United States. 2. Interpersonal conflict. 3. Conflict management. I. Appelbaum Training Institute. II. Title.

LC226.6.A66 2009
371.19'2—dc22   2009010948

This book is printed on acid-free paper.

11   12   13   10   9   8   7   6   5   4   3

Acquisitions Editor:	Jessica Allan
Editorial Assistant:	Joanna Coelho
Production Editor:	Veronica Stapleton
Copy Editor:	Tomara Kafka
Typesetter:	C&M Digitals (P) Ltd.
Proofreader:	Jennifer Gritt
Indexer:	Molly Hall
Cover Designer:	Anthony Paular
Graphic Designer:	Karine Hovsepian

Contents

List of Figures

CHAPTER 6

CHAPTER 7

CHAPTER 8

Preface

Over the years, I have seen Maryln Appelbaum many times speak to audiences on how to handle hard-to-handle people. Her audience members sit transformed as she teaches them the reasons difficult people are difficult and the crucial skills necessary to handle them. The highlight of each session is always a live demonstration on how to handle a difficult parent. I have never seen another speaker do this type of demonstration. Maryln invites the audience to think of the most difficult parent they have ever had to work with and to share examples of what that parent did. Then she chooses the parent example that is the most difficult and invites the audience member who shared the example to come to the stage and pretend to be that parent. Maryln pretends to be the educator and demonstrates the skills to use. The person who is playing the role of the difficult parent always tries to stump Maryln by exaggerating the difficult parent's behavior. She has had parents who rage, complain, whine, and make unreasonable demands. There have been situations that have ranged from silly to dangerous. She always gets the person calm. She always talks to them in a way that they listen. She never allows the difficult person to dominate the situation. Maryln treats each situation with respect and dignity. All her audience members come away having seen in action how to handle hard-to-handle parents.

Maryln Appelbaum is my mother. We have worked together for the past twenty years. She walks her talk. She does this not only with audience members but in real life. This book is packed with the strategies that she teaches at workshops. They work for her. They work for me, and they will work for you. She makes handling hard-to-handle parents easy.

Marty Appelbaum, President of Appelbaum Training Institute

Acknowledgments

Thank you to my son and business partner, Marty Appelbaum. Thank you, Marty, for doing some work I normally do so I could take the time to write this book.

Thank you to our team at Appelbaum Training Institute. You all are a positive force working together to help make a difference in the lives of children and all those who work with them.

Special thanks to my editor, Jessica Allan. Jessica, your patience, your enthusiasm, and your valuable feedback made writing this book easier and better.

Special thanks to the others at Corwin who have been so supportive, most especially Allyson Sharp who is always a positive beacon of light for Corwin.

Additionally, Corwin gratefully acknowledges the following peer reviewers for their editorial insight and guidance:

Raynice Jean-Sigur, PhD
Associate Professor of Early Childhood Education
Kennesaw State University
Kennesaw, GA

Maryann Marrapodi
Chief Learning Officer
Teachscape
New York City, NY

Renee Ponce-Nealon
2005 NBCT/ Kindergarten
McDowell Elementary School
Petaluma, CA

About the Author

 Maryln Appelbaum is well known internationally as an outstanding authority on children, education, and families. She has master's degrees in both psychology and education and completed her doctoral studies in both education and psychology. She has worked as a teacher, an administrator, and a therapist and has been a consultant throughout the United States. She has written more than thirty "how to" books geared exclusively for educators and parents. She has been interviewed on television and radio talk shows and has been quoted in newspapers, including *USA Today*.

She owns a seminar training company, Appelbaum Training Institute, with her son, Marty Appelbaum, and they and their speakers train educators all over the world.

Maryln's influence impacts the entire globe with her thoughts for the day that go out daily to thousands of educators via e-mail. Her strategies have been successfully implemented in schools across the world. There is not a day that goes by that someone does not contact her at Appelbaum Training Institute to tell her "thank you." Those thank-yous come from teachers, administrators, parents, and students whose lives have been impacted by Maryln.

Maryln's books and talks are always packed with strategies for success. She is a positive, motivational, dynamic, caring, one-of-a-kind difference maker for the world.

I dedicate this book to all of the teachers and administrators in the world who work tirelessly to make a difference not only with children but with their families. I also salute the parents who make a difference. Even though this book is written about difficult parents, there are many parents who make educating their children such a pleasure. I also dedicate this book to all of you who work on behalf of children whether it is on television or radio programs or as authors of legislation impacting education. Here's to you all of you who are parents or are parent figures to children—to the special people in this world who

- *Love tirelessly*

- *Plan for the future of children*

- *Share in the joys and in the sorrows of children*

- *Enjoy watching children grow and learn*

- *Make a difference for children in positive ways*

This book is dedicated to you. Together, we all can build bridges to the future for children.

Introduction

I started teaching in the seventies and later became a principal. My background was not only in education but also in psychology. I like to think of myself as a "reasonable" person, and I assumed that the parents of my students would also be reasonable people. While I had many parents who were wonderful, those first years were made doubly tough by having to learn how to handle parents who were often unreasonable. I can still remember the first hard-to-handle parent, Mrs. Walter.* She had five children in the school. All of the children came in each day looking like they needed a bath. Their clothing was often tattered and filthy, and they had body odors that made the other students not want to sit next to them. Mrs. Walter would bring them to school sometimes early and sometimes late, but rarely on time. There was no school bus in those days to come and pick the children up after school, and many times, Mrs. Walter showed up late to pick up her children. When she wanted something, she would just barge in demanding whatever it was that was her latest request. I tried speaking to her over and over again, resolving each time that I would find a way to get through to her. Each time I failed! Eventually, she moved, but other parents came with other problems that took her place. I thought my background in psychology working in a mental hospital had prepared me for handling any kind of situation with difficult people, but it had not! I soon found out that parents were totally different. They had a major investment—their children's futures—and while some parents acted like they didn't care, others wanted to protect that investment and "stay on top of things."

I had no idea how to build a parent team so that they would want to cooperate. I had no clue on how to talk so they would listen. I didn't know how to assert myself and stand up for what was important. It took years and years of both practice and extensive education to acquire the skills to talk to parents so they listen, to build powerful partnerships with parents, and to create an atmosphere that was parent friendly. That is what this book is about. The skills you will learn in this book will help you handle not only difficult parents but all difficult people. You will learn how to

1

prevent hard-to-handle situations before they even develop, how to handle difficult parents and situations with ease, how to listen so parents tell you what is really going on, how to talk to parents so they listen to you, how to hold effective conferences that will help prevent problems before they happen, how to build cooperative partnerships with parents, and how to reach difficult parents and turn them from hard-to-handle to easy-to-handle.

*Name changed.

How to Reach Parents and Prevent Problems Before They Happen

1

The greatest inheritance parents and teachers leave, are children.

—Maryln Appelbaum

THE CHANGING FACE OF FAMILIES

Educators tell me that students have changed. They say that children today are often disrespectful, irresponsible, and rebellious. I tell them that children have not changed, but childhood has changed. I believe that is the same with parents. Parents have not changed. They still love their children and want the best for their children, but parenthood has changed.

The face of the typical family unit has changed. When I was raising my two children, it was a mostly two-parent family world. People got married in their early twenties and had an average of two children. Most women stayed home and raised their children. Men went to work and were the breadwinners. Slowly over the years, this picture changed. More and more women joined the workforce. I vividly remember my own reentry into the workforce. I worked and still was in charge of taking care of the home activities, such as dishwashing, cooking, cleaning, getting the children ready for school, and finding adequate care for the children after school. I was exhausted at the end of the day. I still cared about my children and their teachers and school, but I had less time available to go to their schools and be involved. This is often the case with today's parents.

I saw many instances of diverse types of parenthood in my career as a teacher and administrator. There were some two-parent families raising children. More and more, I found that I had single-parent families in which mothers or fathers had custody as well as parents with shared custody. I had grandparents who had either temporary or permanent custody. There were many blended families, and sometimes those blends changed in the course of the child's being in my schools. Parents married, divorced, remarried, and divorced. There were parents, stepparents, and step-grandparents coming to conferences and open houses. There were two-parent families in which both parents were same-sex parents. And there were parents who were separated not because of divorce but because of work. These were parents who were serving in the armed service and parents or stepparents whose spouses were working in another city, state, or even country.

Increasingly, there were parents who spoke little or no English. My own family growing up was like this. I entered kindergarten speaking absolutely no English. I did not even know that my name was Maryln because my name was said in a different language at home. Working with parents who speak little or no English presents its own challenges because many parents are like my parents and embarrassed to come to school even though they want to know what was going on. My own parents were not only embarrassed that they spoke no English but that we were living below the poverty line. When parents with little English-speaking ability do come to school, they may not understand what they hear. They may, in fact, hear something in such a way that that they get upset, and soon a situation can develop in which they become angry and the school perceives the parents as "hard-to-handle."

There are also parents with different parenting styles (Rudney, 2005). There are parents who are authoritative and always having to be in control. Their children rarely get to have a voice in decisions or choices. At the other end of the spectrum, there are parents who are so permissive that their children are in charge. These parents may be passive with their children, but often they may be aggressive in defending their children, refusing to see that their children have done anything wrong even when it is flaunting them in the face. There are parents who are nurturing, and there are parents who are neglectful.

There are parents who desperately wanted to have children, and there are parents who resent that they have children. There are parents who are good listeners, and there are parents who have no idea how to listen to their children. There are families that are TV families whose only time together is gathered around the television. They eat in front of the television. They talk on the phone while watching television, and they make all their important decisions in front of that television. At the other end of the spectrum, there are families who do not even own a television or a computer. There are parents who are physically ill, mentally ill, alcoholic, or drug addicted (Rudney, 2005). Every parent is different. They are different even when they look alike. That is because every individual is different. Regardless of their differences, it has been my experience that all parents, in their own way, love their children.

Think about this. There is training to do most work, but for the most important work of all, to be a parent, there is absolutely no training. There is only the experience that each person has had growing up. Parents often vow to be different from their own parents, but without training, many fall back into patterns that they learned from their role models. Their parents also loved them and did the best they could do. Parents love their children and are doing the best they can, but without training, most parents are fated to repeat what they learned growing up, like it or not.

Throughout this book, whenever I speak of parents, I will be speaking about all types of family units and all types of parents.

WHAT PARENTS WANT FROM TEACHERS

Teachers Who Know and Care About Children

The number one thing all families want for their children in school is teachers who know and care about their children (Rudney, 2005). Mrs. Green was Jordan's mother. Jordan was an only child. The Greens had tried to conceive for four years when they finally had Jordan. Jordan was very tiny for his age and had had a series of childhood illnesses that had left their mark on this little family. Mrs. Green was concerned about Jordan's new elementary school. I asked her what she wanted for Jordan. She told me that she wanted to be sure that his teachers liked him. She said that if his teachers liked him, he would like them. She said he was so special to her and her husband, and she wanted him to be special to his teachers too, not just one of many students in the class.

Ali was a high school student. She had good grades and was one of those students who worried when assignments weren't turned in on time. Her parents never came to school. I often wondered about that. Ali got really ill and was hospitalized. When I visited her in the hospital, I met her mother and realized that she spoke limited English. An uncle was there who spoke really good English, and he was our interpreter. He explained to me that Ali was embarrassed to have her parents come to school, and that is why they did not come. They cared very much for Ali and were very proud of her good grades. Ali was like many other teens, who prefer that parents do not come to school even when they *are* fluent in English.

The point of these stories is that all parents want their children to be noticed and to be cared for. They want their children treated fairly and respectfully (Rich, 1998). It doesn't matter if their children are preschoolers, elementary students, or secondary students. They know their children will be part of a larger group, and they want to ensure that their children are not just a number, but someone who is special. They want teachers who care—*really care*—about their children. They want teachers to be knowledgeable, but first and foremost, they want to know that their children are cared for by their teachers.

Caring, Calm Classrooms

Parents want their children to be in classrooms in which teachers know and care about teaching (Rich, 1998). They want teachers who encourage their children to learn, teachers who set attainable learning goals, teachers who understand how to teach, and teachers who know how to reach students. They become upset when they hear that other children in the classroom disrupt the class and that children are not paying attention and learning.

Safety

Safety is another major concern of parents (Rich, 1998). Almost every parent at some time or another has seen video clips of school shootings. Parents fear that this can happen. Recently, in the Houston area, where I live, there were two terrorist threats. People who knew about these threats were worried. Some parents did not feel safe sending their children to school.

Parents also fear that their children will be victims of bullies and gangs. They want to know that their children are safe on their way to school, at school, and at the end of the day. That means that they are concerned for their children's safety not only while they are at school but also while they walk or ride the bus to or from school.

Communication With Parents

Most parents want to communicate with teachers (Rich, 1998). They want to hear how their children are doing. They do not like to be surprised. Mr. Kentrall told me a story about his son, Lanny. Lanny had Attention Deficit Hyperactive Disorder (ADHD). It was not diagnosed until Lanny got into middle school. The differences in middle school—which meant changing classes, walking through crowded hallways, having different teachers for different classes—contributed to Lanny's having problems focusing and paying attention. Mr. Kentrall took Lanny to a psychiatrist who diagnosed his son and started him on medication to help alleviate symptoms. When Mr. Kentrall attended the open house at the beginning of the school year, he met Lanny's teachers. They were very busy, but

Mr. Kentrall came away with the impression that Lanny was doing fine. When the first report card came out, Lanny was failing math and history. Mr. Kentrall was stunned and angry. He wished he had known earlier so that he could have worked together with Lanny's teachers to help his son. He could not understand how Lanny's progress could change so quickly. Lanny's teachers did not communicate after the open house. If they had communicated, Mr. Kentrall would not have become so angry.

The ideal way to have prevented Mr. Kentrall from getting upset would have been for his teachers to stay in touch with him throughout that first grading period. At the school open house, his teachers could have told Mr. Kentrall positive points about Lanny and then also added any concerns about math and history. Later on during the same grading period, Lanny's teachers might have contacted Mr. Kentrall and updated him on Lanny's progress. Together, they might have worked out a plan so that Lanny did not receive failing grades. If they did not have time to call, they could have sent him an e-mail telling him options that were available to help Lanny.

REASONS PARENTS DO NOT COME TO SCHOOL

Too Much to Do Barriers

It's difficult to reach and establish relationships with parents who do not come to school. There are many reasons that parents choose to not come to school. The most pressing reason is that they simply are so busy. They have great intentions but then have to work late, have to travel out of town for work, or may have so many other responsibilities that they just cannot come to school.

Language Barriers

There are parents who have limited English who sometimes do not come to school. This is often misinterpreted as lack of concern for their children (Yan, 2006). Cantu's parents came from another country. They spoke very little English. When they came to school and met with her teachers, they did not understand what was being said. They felt out of place and embarrassed. It seemed to them that everyone else knew what was happening. Even though they loved Cantu very much, they eventually stopped going and instead, asked her to tell them what was happening.

Single-Parent Barriers

More than thirty percent of all children in the United States live in single-parent homes (Lee, Kushner, & Cho, 2007). The single parent has increased responsibilities within the home. In an intact family, there can be a division of responsibilities. In the single-parent home, the responsibility belongs exclusively to that one parent. These responsibilities can be extremely time-consuming to the point of lack of parental involvement in the school. Students from single-parent families do not do as well in school academically as those from intact families (Lee et al., 2007). This may be because the single parent is so tired at the end of the day that it takes a lot of effort to ensure homework is done. It is just often easier to take the child's word that everything is fine.

Mrs. Carter has three children ages, fourteen, ten, and two years old. Her husband left when she was pregnant with the third child. She has not heard or received any financial support from him since he left. She has a great job as an executive secretary, and she is terrified of losing her job. When her company asks her to work longer hours, she does. Each night when she finally arrives home, she is exhausted but still has to deal with cooking dinner, getting the kitchen cleaned, packing lunches for the next day, doing emergency loads of wash, and trying to find time to be with each of her children. She wants more than anything to just put her feet up on the sofa and "veg out" for a few hours watching TV, and some evenings she feels lucky when she actually gets to do that. It's a huge sacrifice for her to come to school. It isn't that she doesn't love her children; it's just that she is so preoccupied with survival that it is difficult.

Negative Experiences Barriers

There are some parents who don't come to school because their own experiences in school were negative. I remember one parent telling me, "I hate being here. It reminds me of when I was a child." This parent went on to tell me that when he was a child, he was always in trouble. He was in and out of the principal's office. He said that now, he just doesn't want to go anywhere near the school.

Diversity Barriers

Parents may not come to school because they feel like they are a minority and are not sure if they will be valued or respected (Smrekar & Cohen-Vogel, 2001). Sadly, in some cases this may be true. Parents who are different in any way from the majority of teachers and the school population may feel that their opinions do not count, so why bother to go to school. These parents along with all parents and family types need to be valued for their diversity, and their voices need to be heard.

I told you earlier about my own parents who spoke almost no English. They were embarrassed to come to school for many reasons. Because we were living in a very low-income area, they were very aware that their clothing was different. We all wore the hand-me-downs from other family members and friends. In our community, stories had been shared of other parents who tried with their limited English to stand up for their children in school and were not well received.

Diversity even in these modern times plays an important role in whether or not families feel included. I have one family member who is Native American. He is a "gentle giant." He has been stopped at different times by the police for suspicious activity simply because he looks different.

Parents with physical or mental handicaps also feel different and may fear coming to school. These include parents in wheelchairs, parents missing limbs, parents with visual impairments, and parents with disorders like depression, anxiety, and Asperger's Syndrome which can impair effective communication.

Student Preferences

Students in elementary school generally have no preference about whether or not their parents come to school. Once they get into middle and high school, this sometimes changes. Their parents want them to be more independent, and the students want this independence. These parents become less involved and give their children the opportunity to handle things themselves. Some students carry this need to be independent quite far and become embarrassed or even resentful when their parents come to school. Parents who are struggling to maintain a relationship with their teens may find it easier to stay home.

PREVENT PROBLEMS BEFORE THEY HAPPEN

The best way to prevent problems before they happen is to establish caring relationships with parents. It is very important to create situations in which parents want to come to school and want to be involved. This will affect all aspects of learning for their children including their achievement. Student achievement is higher when parents and educators work in partnership to help children (Lee et al., 2007). In Chapter 8, you will learn many strategies to create those partnerships. The partnership is the "marriage." Courtship comes before marriage, and the remainder of this chapter is filled with strategies to help you "court" parents so that they want to come to school, and they want to be in a partnership. Pick and choose the ones that work best for your school and your situation.

Start in the Neighborhoods

If parents won't come to the school, bring the school to them! Hold meetings in nearby churches in the parents' neighborhoods. Tell them about events happening in the school. Ask local clergypersons to help by making announcements at services and to encourage family members to attend meetings.

Have translators available for neighborhoods where English is limited. Train the translators to be motivational and inspiring. Ensure that they are individuals who are excited about motivating parents to become involved in school. Have them tell parents all the options open to them with English as their second language.

Make the meetings fun. Get food and door prizes donated from local vendors. Have fun activities for the whole family like face painting and games. Assign parent pals who can be translators for those with little or no English-speaking skills.

Make Home Visits

Home visits are an excellent way of building bonds between families and the school. They are time-consuming because it means meeting only one family at a time, and sometimes, it can even be potentially dangerous depending on the neighborhood. I made home visits when I had difficult students whose parents would not come to the school. The first time I ever did this was with the family of a student who was extremely defiant. I had invited the parents to come in to talk to me. They did not show up. I had phoned to speak to them, and they were always busy and going to call me back but never did. Finally, I sent a letter that I would be coming to visit. I followed it up with several messages on their voice mail. I believe that they were stunned when I showed up on their doorstep to talk to them about Jason. The first thing that I remember about that visit was the noise coming from their home. Their windows were open, and there was shouting and the sounds of chaos. They had three sons. The mother opened the door looking totally exhausted. Behind her, two of the boys were chasing each other through the house dressed in their dad's business clothing with shirts dragging over the floors. Two dogs were barking and chasing the boys. Jason, the oldest of the boys, was standing near his mom in total shock. He was stunned to see his teacher in his house. It reminded me of when I have bumped into any of my students at the supermarket or other stores, and they look at me as if to say, "What are you doing here? You are supposed to only be in the classroom!"

Jason's mom, Mrs. Donnelson, invited me into the house. We sat down in her kitchen while the boys and dogs were running around the house.

She told me that she felt like a total failure. I learned that she was a medical doctor who had given up her career to be a stay-at-home mom. She said she didn't come to school conferences or functions because she was terrified she would hear bad news about her boys. She talked and talked. I think she had been holding in her feelings for a long time. I gave her some tips on setting boundaries with the boys, and together, we came up with a plan for Jason. I also recommended some books that would help her manage her boys better. When I left, the house was still chaotic, but she was calmer. She had a plan. Jason's behavior slowly and steadily improved at school.

That was the first of many home visits I made. Almost all of the families I visited were embarrassed about some aspect of their lives, and that appeared to be what had prevented them from coming to school. There were families in which one of the parents was in jail, families in which both parents disappeared and the grandmother was raising the children, families living in extreme poverty. There was one family living in a two-room small home with no electricity and seven family members. This family spoke no English, so I took an interpreter with me. In every case, when families saw my efforts to reach out to them, they became more involved in the academic lives of their children, and it was reflected in their children's academic achievement.

Make Phone Calls

At the beginning of the school year, take time to call each family. Introduce yourself by telling them a few characteristics about yourself. Include your goals for the school year for each child. Have a smile on your face and enthusiasm in your voice. Invite them to share with you their concerns as well as their goals for their children. When you connect in a positive way at the beginning of the school year, it tells parents that you are upbeat and positive in nature. It also helps if you can tell them something positive about their children. It paves the way for a good school year and helps foster parental involvement.

If you call a family that does not appear to speak English, call again with a translator. I have used translators who are other teachers or trained parents to do this. They enjoy helping parents become connected.

Send Introduction Letters

An introduction letter can serve several purposes. It tells the parents a little bit about you and your goals for the coming school year. It also can be used for the purpose of getting parents involved. Be sure to get the letter translated for those families that cannot read English (see Figures 1.1 and 1.2).

Figure 1.1

Sample Introduction Letter (Elementary School)

Dear family of _____,

I am your child's teacher. I am very excited about this new school year. I am looking forward to a wonderful year working with your child.

I would be glad to have your help this year. Please look at the bottom of this letter and let me know if you have any of the following interests, and have your child return the letter to me.

Working together as a team, we will ensure a wonderful school year for your child.

Sincerely yours,

Teacher's signature _____

_____

(Parent) My child's name is _____

My name is _____

You can reach me during the day at (___) _____

and evenings at (___) _____

My e-mail address is _____

I can help in the following ways:

❑ Class trips
❑ Volunteering as a mentor for students who need extra help
❑ Baking or buying treats for the class
❑ Paperwork
❑ Making materials
❑ Contacting other parents
❑ Speaking to the class on _____
❑ Serving as a translator for parents who do not speak English

I speak the following languages: _____

_____

_____

Other ways I can help:

_____

_____

_____

_____

Figure 1.2

Sample Introduction Letter (Secondary School)

Dear family of _____,

I am your child's teacher. I am very excited about this new school year. I am looking forward to a wonderful year working with your child.

I would be glad to have your help this year. Please look at the bottom of this letter and let me know if you have any of the following interests, and have your child return the letter to me.

Working together as a team, we will ensure a wonderful school year for your child.

Sincerely yours,

Teacher's signature _____

_____

(Parent) My child's name is _____

My name is _____

You can reach me during the day at (___) _____

and evenings at (___) _____

My e-mail address is _____

I can help in the following ways:

❑ Volunteering as a mentor for students who need extra help
❑ Making telephone calls to other parents when needed
❑ Paperwork
❑ Making materials at home
❑ Coming to school and making materials for the classroom
❑ Helping during parent nights
❑ Community actions that benefit the school
❑ Serving as a translator for parents who do not speak English

I speak the following languages: _____

_____

_____

Other ways I can help:

_____

_____

_____

_____

Family-Friendly Welcoming Atmosphere

Help families feel welcome when they come to school. Have you ever been invited to a large party at someone's home? There are some homes where you feel great about being there even before you walk in the door. There are other homes where you count the hours and minutes until you can safely leave. The difference is typically in the genuineness and welcoming atmosphere of the homes. It is the same with schools. The more parents feel welcome, the more they will be happy that they are there and involved on behalf of their child.

Welcome Signs

Start by helping families feel welcome as soon as they pull up to the school. Have signs in the parking lot that designate a special area for families to park their cars (Henderson, Mapp, Johnson, & Davies, 2007). Add welcoming words in different languages that reflect the diversity of the school, as in Figure 1.3 (Bergmann, Brough, & Shepard, 2008). When they enter the building and classrooms, have more welcoming signs.

Figure 1.3

Sample Parent Welcome Sign in English

Sherman Oakes School

welcomes families.

"Together we are a partnership to

build a better world for all of our

students."

The Faculty

I remember going into my grandson's school for the first time. His mother was ill, and I was the one who was in charge of getting him enrolled. It was a large high school. Even though my background was an educator, I felt intimidated. I entered the building and walked into the office. Everyone was busy, but someone immediately looked up, smiled, and said, "Hi, how can I help you?" I immediately felt better. Everyone at that school made me feel welcome. When I called on the phone, the same thing happened. It was a pleasure to become involved in my grandson's education with that school.

When parents walk into your school, ensure that they are welcomed warmly by faculty. Parents can feel if they are welcome, and that helps to ensure that parents want to come back.

Welcome Notes From Students

Make welcome notes for all families (Boult, 2006). Have the students participate in making them. The students each write several sentences telling parents about their new schedule or something about their class. Include a few drawings by students. Make sure that each student contributes to this project so that parents can look for their child's work and name beside it. It's a great way to start the school year involving both students and parents. Figure 1.4 has some sayings that were included in one elementary school's welcome notes. Students in secondary schools can also write welcome notes to their parents.

Figure 1.4

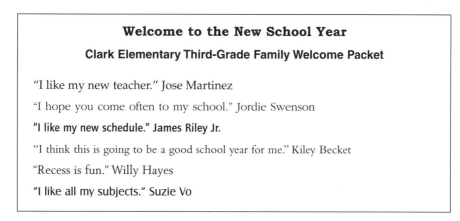

Welcome to the New School Year

Clark Elementary Third-Grade Family Welcome Packet

"I like my new teacher." Jose Martinez

"I hope you come often to my school." Jordie Swenson

"I like my new schedule." James Riley Jr.

"I think this is going to be a good school year for me." Kiley Becket

"Recess is fun." Willy Hayes

"I like all my subjects." Suzie Vo

MAKING DIVERSE GROUPS FEEL WELCOME

At one time, I owned several private schools. I made it a requirement that when parents wanted to enroll their children, they had to first visit and observe the classrooms. I often heard comments afterward about the diversity of the students. The truth is that I never thought about it. For me, a student was a student. I looked more at how diverse the individual students were in terms of learning needs then in terms of a child's appearance or socioeconomic status.

While that was my perspective, it is not necessarily the perspective of parents. Parents look for children who are similar to their own children. They look for other parents who are similar to them. They fear that their children will stand out in a negative way. It is important to make all parents and all children feel welcome. Here are some ways to welcome diverse populations and make them more comfortable.

Translation Buddies

Use parent volunteers to help translate information for parents who speak little or no English (Boult, 2006). Have them translate all letters to the parents' native tongue and also have them contact parents by telephone and speak to them in their native language.

My company does seminars throughout the United States. Sometimes, we are notified ahead that there will be an individual attending who is hearing impaired and has requested a sign-language interpreter. We always accommodate this need. It is interesting to me that while people think about making accommodations for those who are hearing impaired, people don't typically think of making accommodations for people who speak very little English, and do not understand what is being said. When you have parent nights, make sure that there is someone to greet parents in their own native language and translate for them things that are said.

At the beginning of the school year, identify the families who have second-language strengths. Use this information to pair up families based on language ability. For example, a family bilingual in Chinese and English would be paired with another family who spoke Chinese but little or no English. The bilingual family could then translate important school information into Chinese for their school buddies.

For matters of confidentiality, identify other faculty members who have strengths in other languages and have them serve as interpreters. The most important thing is to look for people who parents will trust when they are interpreting for them.

Telephone Tree

Have bilingual parents contact other parents who are not fluent in English to tell them about events occurring in the school and to invite them. Parents sign up for this at the beginning of the year, and then you contact the volunteers when you need help. This is a great strategy to get all parents to come to school, not just for parents who have limited or no English. It is especially effective for passive parents who do not attend functions. It benefits both the volunteers who make the calls because they can do it on their own time at home, and it is a benefit to parents who receive the calls. You can have a prepared script for parents to use when making the calls to ensure there is no miscommunication.

Books

Books are a great resource for parents. Some parents are passive and have a hard time coming to school but enjoy reading and learning. Refer them to books on different topics that are relevant to your school. Secondary schools may offer books on occupations, colleges, and obtaining scholarships. Both elementary and secondary schools can have a recommended list that includes books on communicating with children, getting children to do their homework, and other relevant topics. Find books in languages other than English that bilingual parents can read and share with their children at home.

Wish Lists

Create a wish list for your class and have it translated into the languages of each of your families. Send it home with students. Knowing what teachers need for their classrooms can help build communication between all parties involved. It is a great way for more passive parents to be involved. They may not want to come to school, but they can still feel like they are contributing.

Parents Share Cultures

Find ways to include diverse parents in your classroom. Parents come and share about their holidays. They can also come and share about objects and artifacts from their cultures. It is a great way to open the door to teaching a social studies, geography, or history lesson. You can tie it in to other lessons too in other subjects. It makes parents feel welcome while also benefiting the class. Keep in mind that in secondary school, students whose parents are speaking may be absent that day. Mrs. Rawana was excited about speaking at her son's social studies class. She had signed up when she went to his conference. When the day came for her to go to his school, he said he didn't feel well. She went and spoke to his class. When she came home, he was magically feeling better. He told her several days later that he just didn't want to be there. He was afraid of what his peers would say. Fortunately, they all spoke highly of his mom and what she had shared. This is not always the case. Children can be critical and even cruel about the parents and families of their peers.

OPENING THE DOORS TO THE SCHOOL FOR ALL FAMILIES

Picnics

Picnics are great ways for families to get many parents to the school. It is a safe, easy way to have fun and help parents feel comfortable with school. Depending on the budget, schools can provide the food or families can bring their own food.

Fashion Shows

Fashion shows are a fun way of getting families to come to school. Get local stores involved to provide the clothing. Parents will come to schools to see their children participate in a fashion show. Involve the parents and have them also be models. They will tell their friends, and the more the entire neighborhood realizes that your school is a warm and friendly school, the more it will encourage further family participation.

Thoughts for the Day

I send out daily a thought for the day that is a strategy or inspiration for teachers. Teachers have told me that they pass these thoughts on to their parents. That is another way of helping family members better understand both how important they are in the lives of their children and also gives them strategies for handling childhood issues. You are welcome to subscribe to my thought for the day at www.atiseminars.org or to come up with your own saying or thought for the day. This can be posted on the wall for parents to see, or better still, copied and sent home on a special colored paper every day. Another option is to forward it through e-mail to parents.

Helping Hand Projects

It has been my own experience that even parents who typically do not come to school or get involved in other ways will help others in times of need. Several years ago, a major hurricane struck in Louisiana, and thousands of people fled to Houston. The schools were filled with students whose homes in Louisiana had been destroyed. Schools and teachers sent home notes that they needed support for these families. Children who had little or no clothing poured into Houston-area schools. Family members contributed whatever they could to help those families, including clothing. It created a sense of community to come together to help someone else.

You can use this same theme with your families. Find a cause, something that all the students and family members can help with. Let them all know ways they can help and acknowledge and thank them for coming together as a school community to help others.

Babysitting

I have talked with many families over the years who tell me that they would come to school, but they have no one to watch their children. Provide babysitting for families to enable parents to come to school with their children.

Convenient Times

Schedule all family functions at times that are easier for parents. Have evening functions early in the evenings so that it does not interfere with bedtimes of children. When planning, always think of what will work best for families.

Food

Have you ever heard the saying, "If you feed them, they will come!" The food served does not have to be fancy. It does have to be filling and good. Many times, family members rush to their children's schools after a long day at work. Food provides incentive to get parents to make the journey to their children's schools.

Door Prizes

Have lots of door prizes when parents come to the school (Bergmann et al., 2008). Invite community businesses to donate the door prizes. Have students make door prizes to be given away. It's fun for parents to win prizes and adds an extra incentive to get parents to come to school.

Family Bulletin Boards

Everyone likes to look at photos or articles that represent themselves. Have a family bulletin board in each classroom (Bergmann et al., 2008). Encourage students to bring photos of family events that have themes. Each month change the theme and change the photos. Instead of photos, you can have family quotes. Here are some themes for the family bulletin board:

- Family vacations
- Family fun time
- Family gems (family jokes)
- Family best motivational sayings
- Family favorite foods
- Family favorite movies
- Family favorite songs

Invite students to help design the themes. Encourage them to get their parents involved. The more the families are involved, the more they start wanting to come to school.

Parents as Students

One of the favorite activities of parents at my own schools was a Reversal Night. Parents came to school and participated as students in a modified mini-day. They wore name tags with their children's names. They sat in their children's seats. They got to see their children's work and experience the evening through the eyes of their children. I had nearly one hundred percent participation at this event every year. It was a great way for parents to get to know their children's teachers and to also become more involved with the school because I always had sign-up sheets and made announcements about areas in which we needed help.

A fun activity for secondary schools is to have students write a short introduction about each class for their parents. They give it to their parents before they arrive in the class. My daughter did this for me when she was in high school. It was fun reading her descriptions of her classrooms and her teachers.

Telephone Blitzes

Have a phone blitz where you contact each parent once school has started. Introduce yourself and tell them how happy you are to be working with their child this school year. Keep it upbeat and positive (see Figure 1.5).

Figure 1.5

Sample First Telephone Call

Hi Mrs. Kennedy,

I'm Geraldine Stokes, Josh's new teacher. I just wanted to take a minute to introduce myself. I have lots of great plans for this school term. We will be studying lots of fun subjects including American history, American heroes, and American legends.

I will be sending out notes and e-mails to keep you posted about our class. You can respond to my e-mails too with any concerns that you have.

I'm looking forward to meeting you at the open house in two weeks. Have a great day.

Bye for now.

School Tours

It can be an overwhelming experience for students to start new schools or new classrooms. As part of an orientation to the school, take parents on a visit throughout the school. Use this as an opportunity to get families excited about the school and to encourage them to become involved. The goal is for them to go home and tell their children about the school and what they saw. The enthusiasm of the parents will transmit itself to the enthusiasm of students.

Family Portraits

Taking family portraits is a great way of getting families to come to school. In addition to taking photos of students, invite parents to come and have the entire family take a portrait (Bergmann et al., 2008). Be sure to find a photographer who is very good and also very reasonable. Send out the notices ahead of time and be sure to include the rates as well as the dates.

Class Web Sites

A class Web site can open the door to get parents to peek into classrooms. Families log on to the Web site and see photos of their children as well as read the latest news about what their children are doing. It is a way for parents to be in contact that may entice them to leave their homes and come to the school itself.

Class Newsletters

Class newsletters are a good way to keep parents informed about events in the school and in the lives of their children. Involve older students in writing the newsletters. Keep them short. If they are long, parents may not read them. Include the names of students. Parents enjoy seeing their children's names in print. Make sure to rotate names so that all students get their names in the newsletters at different times. Use a personal approach using words like "we" and "our."

Tell parents what students are learning. I have heard repeatedly from parents that their children usually don't tell them what they are learning. Mrs. Johnson was one of those parents. She told me that that every day she asks her son, Thomas, "What did you learn today?" He has the same response every day, "Nothing." The newsletter is a good way to tell parents highlights about what students are learning. You can involve students by having them draw or diagram something from their favorite learning topic.

Include a section with tips for how parents can help their children. It can be tips for completing homework such as those you will find in Chapter 8.

The goal of the newsletter is to open the doors of communication so that parents will want to come to school and work together as a partnership. If your school is in an area in which it is possible to have your newsletter be paperless, then by all means, go paperless and send it via e-mail.

Informative Lists

Hand out lists for parents (Haviland, 2003). These are special lists, not lists for school supplies. Instead, they are lists that are "must-knows." For example, have lists of ways to help children enjoy reading more, a list of ways parents can get students to do their homework, a list of skills students should have mastered by the time they graduate from your school, and a list of symptoms of alcohol and drug use.

Topics for Parent Meetings

The topic is often the draw to entice parents to come to school. Look for topics that are of high interest to parents. Here are some topics that have been used successfully to get parents to come to schools:

- Ten ways to help your child succeed in school
- The challenges and joys of single parenting
- Living with and loving your teenager
- How to be a strong-willed parent to a strong-willed child
- How to talk to your child about tough topics

- Hassle-free homework
- How to talk so kids will listen
- Getting into college
- How to help your child get higher grades
- How to set limits and stick to them
- Obesity and anorexia: Keeping your child healthy
- Signs of depression in children and what you can do about it
- Underage drinking—what you need to know as a parent

Find your own topics, topics of interest for the families in your school. Use relevant topics. After 9/11, a good topic was how to keep children safe. Parents have to feel that their time was well-spent (Haviland, 2003). Even an hour out of a busy parent's day is a lot. Start and end meetings on time. Parents don't like meetings that drag on well past the time the meeting was scheduled to end. The important thing is to get the parents there. Once they are there, make them feel so welcome that they look forward to coming back. Together, you can make a huge difference on the lives of their children.

Group E-Mails

Stay in touch with families by setting up a group e-mail. This is a wonderful way for parents to know not only about upcoming events but also about assignments. The latter gets more and more important as students get older. It keeps parents in the loop. They know what their children are learning, when they are learning it, and even what assignments need to be turned in and when they are due. Keep the e-mails positive and upbeat.

While this is a great way to reach parents, it will not work if you have parents who do not have e-mail. Those parents will need personal phone calls and pages sent home with their children.

Family Deposits

Children are often close-mouthed with their parents. The more parents know, the more they will be able to carry on meaningful conversations with their children. Tell them about school happenings, information that their often close-mouthed children do not tell them (Haviland, 2003). Send the information home on a special form you create called a family deposit. It is deposited with the family for them to have information about their child's school. Include information such as new faculty members their children will be meeting and new special programs. Include special events their children are excited about such as the basketball team that is on its way to victory or got defeated because their star player broke a leg. The events do not all have to be about sports. In one high school recently, the halls were buzzing with stories about Jed who had been in a horrible traffic accident over the weekend. It's important that families know what is happening that impacts their children.

Parent Deposit Slips

You also need to know about important events in children's home lives. Provide parents with a supply of blank deposit slips on paper of a different color. Tell them to list their "deposits," the things they want the school to know about their child. They may list items such as family illness, the child didn't sleep well the previous night, or anything else they think is relevant for the school to know.

Family Fun

Above all, ensure that all meetings at the school are happy meetings. Parents will strive to take the time to come back when they have had a good time. Set a goal to get each parent more involved and to have each parent feel comfortable coming to the school. The results will amaze you. You will have taken giant steps to create happier parents, and that translates into giant steps to prevent hard-to-handle parents and situations from occurring.

Connect

The strategies in this chapter have all been to help you understand the parents in your school and to find ways to help them become more involved and connected. When you work with students, the more you connect, the less you almost always correct. Students respond better when they feel the connection with their teachers. It is similar with parents. The more they feel a connection, the more they will feel like they are important and that their opinions count. You and the parents have a better chance to become a team working together to help their children, your students. The following chapters will give you great tools to foster that connection with parents who are more difficult. They are powerful strategies that will work for you and for your parents. The end goal is to connect and communicate and build a collaborative team that will benefit the students you teach.

About Hard-to-Handle People

2

Your own mood is more contagious than the flu to others.

— Maryln Appelbaum

WHAT IS A DIFFICULT PERSON?

Have you ever known someone who you generally wanted to avoid? You found that person was just too difficult, and you felt uncomfortable with them. That may have been a difficult person. While everyone can be difficult at times, a truly difficult person is someone whose behaviors cause difficulties for others over and over again. The difficult person is someone who is chronically difficult. Generally, this person is not only difficult with you but with everyone. While it sometimes is easier to avoid some difficult people, you cannot do it with parents. Difficult people are hard-to-handle people. They require special skills and strategies in order for you to work with them successfully as a team.

CHARACTERISTICS OF DIFFICULT PEOPLE

Difficult people often share similar characteristics. Look at the checklist in Figure 2.1 and see if any of the parents of your students have these characteristics.

If you checked off three or more characteristics, then you probably have a hard-to-handle parent in your school. This is especially true if you find yourself walking on eggshells every time you are around the person and feeling intimidated or even frightened, or you respond by getting hostile and angry. Difficult parents can make you feel miserable and can make your work harder.

Figure 2.1

Characteristics of Difficult People

☐ They often complain.

☐ They put others down.

☐ They are not willing to hear thoughts that conflict with their ideas.

☐ They stay in control by putting others down.

☐ They believe their way is the best way.

☐ They are argumentative.

☐ They are stubborn.

☐ They act as if they know all there is about a subject.

☐ They think of all the reasons something will not work.

☐ They may agree to things that they may not support later.

☐ They rush you to make decisions.

☐ They make you feel sorry for them to get what they want.

☐ They let you down.

☐ They may complain to you about someone and then go to that person and complain about you.

☐ Nothing you do is good enough. They always want more.

☐ They are quick to anger.

☐ They are often unpredictable.

☐ They act like they have done nothing wrong.

☐ They may jab at you with put-downs, digs, criticism, and false rumors.

There are some principles of difficult behavior that I have found working with parents that are the same when working with difficult students. First, behavior that is reinforced is more likely to be repeated (Umbreit, Ferro, Liaupsin, & Lane, 2007). That means whenever you give in to a difficult person, that person will think, "This works. I will do it some more."

Second, when you are learning new methods of responding to difficult people, they will be confused at first. This can make them initially escalate the difficult behavior. That does not mean that what you are doing is not going to work. Think it over carefully. If it is a response that shows respect for both yourself and the other person, it probably is still the right response.

Third, and most important, remember that doing nothing is doing something. When you let others treat you as a doormat by doing absolutely nothing about it, you are actually teaching them to continue to act the same way toward you.

It is very important that you have a handle on how to handle hard-to-handle parents. Not only can they make your life miserable, but it will also affect the students. You cannot work together as a team until you can communicate and share solutions with parents. It cannot be "my way or the highway" with these parents because then the highway has too many vehicles going at high speeds in different directions, and the stage is set for a collision course.

THE SIX "NEVERS" WITH HARD-TO-HANDLE PARENTS

1. Never Argue

It's important to never argue with difficult people (Kosmoski & Pollack, 2000). It just escalates the conflict. It creates a win–lose situation. When one of you loses, the student loses too. You cannot be a team and fight. It is like a mother and father that fight over what is right for the child. Even if they are both trying to help the child, the conflict becomes more important than the child. Feelings are hurt. The child loses.

2. Never Get Defensive

When you begin to defend your position, you are automatically saying to the parent, "You are wrong. That is not what I said." It immediately becomes an argument with you trying to prove what you said and the parent then responding.

3. Never Raise Your Voice

The louder your voice becomes, the louder the parent's voice will become (Appelbaum, 2009a). Moreover, when a person yells, the respondent of the yelling goes into "fight or flight" mode. That means the respondent will become more argumentative and fight or withdraw into flight mode and say nothing. The latter is not necessarily good because the respondent still has strong hidden feelings and may eventually explode in some way.

When people are yelled at, they may agree to do whatever is asked but then not do it. They may be so upset from the humiliating experience of having someone yell at them, they may sabotage the yeller or spread rumors or gossip. People may be so hurt that even though they say nothing out loud, they are in a battle with the person who yells, a subtle more invisible fight, and it becomes even more difficult to become a team and work together for the student.

4. Never Say or Do Anything
for Which You Have to Make Amends

One of the most amazing things that can occur when working with difficult parents is that even though they are the ones provoking the situation, you may respond in such a way that *you* are the one who needs to later apologize. Be careful to not use sarcasm or say anything that you later regret saying. It won't help you or the parent, and most of all, it won't help the student.

5. Never Take It Personally

When parents are difficult, it often has absolutely nothing to do with you. It is generally the parent's style of operating. It is a learned behavior that has been used for years. They don't do it only with you. They do it with others too. Don't start thinking, "What did I do to make her not like me?" It is not about liking you. If you take it personally, it will only make it worse.

6. Never Lose Your Cool

Stay calm when talking to difficult parents. If you lose it, the entire situation will deteriorate. Once you lose your temper, you are actually doing all of the other "nevers" too. Mr. Ortega was Bruce's teacher. Bruce's dad, Mr. Padin was extremely hostile, complaining, and argumentative. After listening to Mr. Padin for close to thirty minutes and getting nowhere in the conference, Mr. Ortega found himself getting angrier and angrier. He heard over and over again negative comments. "Your class is horrible. Bruce never got into trouble until he came into your classroom. You are one of the worst teachers my son has ever had. How can you treat him like that? I wish you were dead or at least in an auto accident so that you never came back here, and then my son would get a different teacher." Mr. Ortega listened and listened and listened and listened some more, and then finally, he had had it. He stood up and pounded the table and said, "Shut up! I have listened to you for the past thirty minutes and all you do is complain. No wonder your son has problems. You are the worst excuse of a parent I have ever seen!!"

It is easy to see that Mr. Ortega was provoked; however, he needed to stay calm and not lose his "cool." Students provoke you too, but you have to always stay calm and in charge of the situation with them. You have to do the same thing with parents. Always keep in mind that your goal is to become a team. That means learning to work with even the most difficult parent.

Figure 2.2

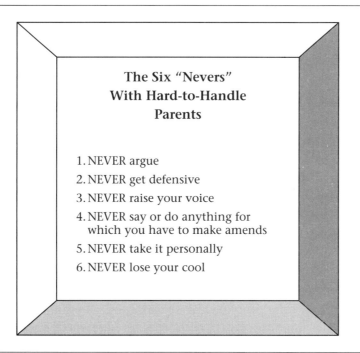

The Six "Nevers"
With Hard-to-Handle
Parents

1. NEVER argue
2. NEVER get defensive
3. NEVER raise your voice
4. NEVER say or do anything for which you have to make amends
5. NEVER take it personally
6. NEVER lose your cool

FIVE WAYS PARENTS CAN MAKE YOU LOSE YOUR COOL AND HOW TO CHOOSE HEALTHIER RESPONSES

1. They Make You Feel Guilty

They make you feel guilty if you do not go along with what they want. If you have ever dealt with hard-to-handle parents, you know that they often complain and complain telling you all the things that you do wrong. You may hear things like it's your fault that their children are not learning. "Payton learned great when he was in other classes. You must be doing something different. His friend, Kent, is learning in his class." There may be some truth in what the parent is saying, and your teaching style may not match Payton's learning style; however, it may also be that the parent just does not want the child to take responsibility for lack of effort. If you believe that you are doing a thorough job with the student, then the parent's comments are designed to make you feel guilty so you do more for their child. While I believe that it is important to do everything you can for each child you teach, I also believe that you have to teach children to do things independently. If you know that you are doing everything you can possibly do for the student, do not succumb to the guilt. Instead respond to the parent by saying, "I am sorry you feel that way. Let's assume that I was doing everything to help your child learn, and there were still problems. Do you have any ideas for me to use to get Payton more motivated? I would really enjoy your input."

This establishes a framework for working together as a team. You are avoiding the six "nevers" and gently steering the parent back to the issue.

2. They Make You Feel Sorry for Them

There are some people who use being a "victim" to get others to do things for them. In reality, there really are people who have been victimized at some point in their lives. I am not speaking about those people. Those are people who need help. For example, people who have fled a hurricane and cannot return home need help. Women who are in abusive relationships and are doing everything they can to get out of the relationship and keep their children safe need help. I am not speaking about the countless true stories of people who genuinely need help but about those people who use victim tales to manipulate others to get them to do things for them. Here is an example of a parent using a victim story. Mrs. Benson said to Tyler's teacher, "I have so much to do that it's been hard to keep up with managing Tyler's homework. It takes me hours at night to unwind after having to work all day and then come home at night to cook dinner. I am a single parent and exhausted, and then I have to find the time to do my hair, polish my nails, find the perfect clothing for the next day, pack a lunch for us, and still find time to watch my favorite TV programs each night to unwind. I'm so tired that I could get sick." While some of what you may hear is actually true, sometimes, it's just a way to get you to do something for them that they don't want to do. In this case, Mrs. Benson did not want to be involved in her child's schoolwork.

When I worked as a therapist, I developed a saying, "Victims create victims" because over and over again I saw this happen in relationships. Catherine was a private school principal. She had a mom who told her one sob story after another about all the reasons she could not pay the tuition. Catherine let the child stay in her school without tuition for several months, growing more and more upset with the situation. Finally, she told the mother that she no longer could keep the child without tuition. Instead of being grateful for the months that her child had gone for free, the mother got irate. Later Catherine learned that this mother had pulled the same scam with other schools too.

When people attempt to make you feel sorry for them, you can apologize (Jaksec, 2003). You can say, "I am so sorry to hear that. It sounds like you have some problems. However, there is still another problem, and this one can grow to be bigger, or with your help, it can become smaller. I have some ideas for ways we can team up to help Tyler. I would like to share them with you and hear your ideas to help him too."

Once again, you have avoided the six "nevers." More important, you have found a way to acknowledge the parent's problems and still establish communication and teamwork to help the child succeed.

3. They Rush You

Parents often rush you so that you are pressured to make decisions you might not ordinarily make. I have seen parents rush into a room with a problem and want something done right then—that minute. The teacher or the administrator who is in the midst of important work feels rushed and overwhelmed and quickly says, "OK." It worked!

Connie Masters was in the midst of teaching her class. She had presented the lesson and was now walking around checking the different groups that were all working on assignments at differing levels. As she walked around the room, she noticed that one group of students was having a difficult time. She sat down with them to reteach the lesson using a different teaching style when suddenly her door burst open, and there was Cory's dad, Mr. Robinson. Mr. Robinson spotted her and quickly went over to her and said, "I need you to make a decision right now about Cory." Suddenly, the calm lesson and quiet atmosphere of the room changed into chaos. Connie felt pressured to make a decision right away and get Mr. Robinson out of her classroom.

When you are feeling rushed and pressured to make a decision and you are not ready, it's important to stop before you say something you later regret. Tell the parent that you need time to think about it. "I'm going to need to think about it. I will need to get back to you."

Once a word has been spoken, it can never be taken back. Once you have said something in haste, it can have later ramifications for you, the student, and the parent. When you tell the parent you will get back later, you are taking steps toward building a team.

4. They Use Manipulation

Have you ever read articles in the paper in which people were conned out of money? Those people were manipulated in some way to give up what they wanted. There are some people who have been victims of land deals in which they thought they got some kind of instant bargain but instead got a huge burden. Parents are people. They are not generally con artists. They are instead people who want very much what they deem is appropriate for their children. To get what they want, they may do things that they would not otherwise do. If you ever feel manipulated, chances are, it is really happening. Instead of using one of the six "nevers," you need to have appropriate words to use to stop the manipulation and to get on with helping the student. Respond to the parent who you feel is manipulating you by saying, "Your child is important to me, and I want to help you. You have ideas for your child, and I do too. Let's brainstorm solutions, you and I, so that we can together make a difference for your child. Here's some paper, and we can start with your ideas. Then I will tell you mine. Together, we will find the ones that work best for your child. We can get started right now. Is that OK with you?"

This strategy allows parents to have a voice in what they want, but at the same time, it ends manipulation and starts cooperation.

5. They Make You Feel Frustrated, Anxious, Upset, Angry, Inferior, or Negative

It is easy to get really upset and feel some negative emotions when you are dealing with difficult parents. However, it is vital that you do not express those feelings. Instead, know that the parent is not making you feel the feeling. You are choosing to feel the feeling. Yes, that is right. It is your choice. For example, three people may be sitting at a restaurant. They have all ordered the same entrée. They are all hungry. They sit there chatting, eating some bread and butter, drinking some water or a soft drink. Fifteen minutes goes by, and there is still no order. Thirty minutes goes by, and there is still no food. Forty-five minutes goes by, and there is still no food. An hour goes by, and the food is finally delivered by the waiter. The food is cold. One person at the table is so hungry and says, "I'm starved" and digs in and starts eating. Another person says, "This food is cold. I'm going to send it back and get it heated." The third person stands up and speaks loudly so that all heads turn to face the table, "This is ridiculous. I waited an hour and then the food comes and it is cold. We need to get our money back and leave." The same situation happened to all three people, yet they all made different choices about how they would feel and, more important, how they would respond. It is the same with you handling the difficult parent. You cannot control what the difficult person says, but you sure can control how you will respond. You are in charge of your own emotions. No one can make you feel an emotion. They can try, but then it is your choice how you will respond.

You cannot handle difficult parents unless you are calm (Sanderson, 2005). That is an important key to success. You need to stay in charge of your own emotions especially when someone else is out of control with their emotions. The more you know about your methods of responding, the better you will be able to handle situations when they arise. Figure 2.3 is a quiz that will help you recognize your own tendencies. Check off the top five items that describe your actions in challenging situations.

Knowledge is power. The more you know about yourself, the better you will be able to handle hard-to-handle parents. Look over the areas from the little self-test and decide which areas you want to improve. Write them down. Also look at your strengths. The more you recognize your own patterns, the more you will be able to improve them.

Figure 2.3

How Do I Handle Challenging Situations?

❑ I get easily impatient.

❑ When I am displeased with someone, I may shut down communication and withdraw.

❑ I feel inwardly annoyed when family and friends do not comprehend my needs.

❑ When I talk about my irritations, I really do not want to hear an opposite point of view.

❑ I never forget when someone does something wrong.

❑ I have been told that I have a bad temper.

❑ I may be quiet at the time I am annoyed, but I always get the person back in some way.

❑ I enjoy confrontations.

❑ When someone is annoyed with me, I jump easily into conflict.

❑ I have a tendency to be harsh with others, especially when I am in a leadership role.

❑ Although I may not be right, I sometimes blame others for my problems.

❑ Sometimes I lose my temper and feel badly afterward.

❑ I am not always sensitive to the needs of others.

❑ I get quiet and say nothing.

❑ I let others bulldoze me.

❑ I am patient.

❑ I am tactful.

❑ I try to see the other person's side as well as my own.

How to Handle the 3
Hard-to-Handle Parent

Strategies for Success

Communication is more than talking; it is an art.

—Maryln Appelbaum

Nearly three-quarters of teachers say that parents treat them as adversaries (Gibbs, 2005). They want to have better relationships with parents, but it is difficult when they are treated this way. This chapter is packed with strategies for you to handle hard-to-handle parents. Some strategies may fit your personality better than others. They are all effective. Choose the ones that are most appropriate for your unique personality and the hard-to-handle parent.

THE RIGHT WAY TO SAY "NO"

There are ways to say "no" to a parent who is hostile and demanding that can escalate or de-escalate the situation. Here are some strategies that enable you to say "no" in ways that will de-escalate potential conflicts.

Ask for Time to Think

When parents catch you off guard with a request that you feel is completely inappropriate, delay responding. This gives you the chance to calm down and reflect. You may even change your mind about how you want to handle the situation. In the heat of the moment, it is easy to say something that you later regret. Parents may also back down once they have had time to think. Say something like this:

"Let me think about that and get back to you _____." (time frame)

"Yes, I can see that's important to you. I need to think about it and will get back to you _____." (time frame)

Use the Sandwich Technique

Sometimes, you have to tell a parent "no." The sandwich is a tactful way of doing this. A sandwich is composed of two pieces of bread with an ingredient inside such as meat. The two pieces of bread are represented by two positive statements. One is used at the beginning of the strategy, and the other is used at the end of the strategy. The inside ingredient is the meat. It is your tactfully phrased "no." Here is an example of a teacher responding to a parent's request that her son take time off from doing homework.

Bread: *It's neat that you are so concerned about your son.*

The Ingredient: *It will not work for him to take time off and not do any homework. He would fall behind the other students.*

Bread: *Thank you so much for your concern. We both want him to succeed.*

Say "Yes" and Offer Choices

It's important to find ways to say "no," so that it is not offensive to parents. The sandwich is one way to do this. Another way to do this is to say "yes" and offer choices. For example, a parent comes to you and makes an inappropriate request for his son. Here is how you can say "yes" when you really mean "*no.*"

"Yes, that is one method for your son. The school policy is to do the following in this situation. (Name alternatives.) Which one do you prefer?"

This is a great way to say "no" because it actually empowers parents. They are involved and contributing to a decision to help their child.

THE OPPOSITE RESPONSE FOR PARENTS WHO ARE NEGATIVE AND ARGUMENTATIVE

I have used the opposite response effectively for many years. I first noticed how effective it was with children and then later modified it for use with adults. Here's a scene that may seem familiar to you using the opposite response with children. Mrs. Paulson told her two-year-old son Charlie that it was time to go to bed. He started crying and said, "No!" She said, "Fine! You will have to stay up all night." He again started crying and said, "No, I want to go to bed." Saying the opposite produced the results that Mrs. Paulson wanted for her son. While that example was of a preschooler, it often is the same with teenagers. They want very much to assert their independence. Corrine was sixteen years old, and she thought her mother was old-fashioned and out of touch with the way things are in the world now. She argued with her mother over almost everything. Corrine always had to have the last word, and it was always the opposite of what her mother said. Her mother thought about this, and one day she tried the opposite response. She told Corrine she hoped she would go to a football game that Friday night instead of staying home for family night. Her mother really preferred for Corrine to stay home with the family. When Corrine heard her mom tell her to go to the game, she said, "No, this is one Friday night that I decided to do the family night routine!"

Here is an example of the opposite response with a parent. Paden's mother, Mrs. Marshall, was meeting with his teacher, Ms. Caldwell. Ms. Caldwell was feeling badgered. It seemed like anything she said was wrong and turned into a potential argument. Finally, Ms. Caldwell said, "Mrs. Marshall, you are right that this is not working out. I don't want to argue with you, so we have several choices. We can brainstorm solutions for the issue and write them all down and then come up with one that is mutually acceptable, or we can delay this meeting for another time. Which do you want?" Mrs. Marshall looked at her and realized that the conversation had been going nowhere, and said, "Let's brainstorm solutions. I think that will be fine."

There were no more arguments. By confronting the situation and saying the opposite of what Mrs. Marshall expected, which was an argument, Mrs. Caldwell transformed the situation. She had also empowered Mrs. Marshall while setting boundaries that said, "We will not continue like this." It was a "win–win" for everyone. She had taken control of that situation, and that is what you need to do too.

REPETITION RESPONSE

I recently rented a DVD, but I did not realize that it had a scratch on the bottom. I was excited to see the movie. I pushed the play button, and the first minute was fine. Then it paused, and it replayed what I had just seen. I hit play, and it did it again. It just kept replaying what I had already seen. I took the DVD out and noticed that the bottom of it was scratched.

While the movie never did work, repeating over and over again something is sometimes necessary in a conversation with a difficult person. Here is an example of the first time I used the repetition strategy. It was not with a parent, but with a motel manager that was trying to overcharge my family. It was a tiny hotel in Florida, and my family and I were ready to go back home. I went to the front desk and asked for my bill. I looked it over and saw that it was more than the nightly rate we had been promised. The front desk manager knew we were in a hurry to leave for our trip back home, and I think he thought we would overlook it. I showed him the bill and explained that we had been guaranteed a different rate. He insisted that we pay the greater rate. I repeated that we had been guaranteed a different rate. I showed him the paper with the guarantee. He continued to insist that we owed the greater rate. I held my ground and said that we had a guaranteed rate, and we were happy to pay that rate. When he saw that I was not going to be worn down and would stay for as long as it took, he finally said, "You're right." When it was all over, I wondered how many times he had done this same thing to other people, who had finally given up.

It is the same with parents. They may have become accustomed to getting the response they want. They think they only have to hold out, and it will happen, and many times they are right. Educators often think, "Let's just do whatever it takes to get them off our backs." When you use the repetition response, they realize that this is not going to work.

DON'T GET SIDETRACKED

One way that parents sometimes get what they want is that they keep changing the argument. They shift and bring up other issues, and it seems like the situation is getting worse and worse. Finally, the teacher may give in just to stop all the other issues from developing into an argument too.

It is important to not get sidetracked. Instead, stay firm in what you want and need. Stick to the issues. Do this tactfully and firmly.

"That is interesting. Let's talk about resolving _____ first. Do you have any new solutions on which we both can agree?"

AGREE WITH THE PERSON

When the parent is argumentative, you can take the wind out of their sails by agreeing with them. There is almost always something in what they are saying that is true. That does not mean that you do what they want. Here is how it works. The parent complains, and you say,

"You may have a point. Now I would like for you to hear my point too, and together we will come up with a solution that works for your child."

APOLOGIZE

When the parent is angry and hostile, it is sometimes appropriate to apologize (Jaksec, 2003). This does not mean you are sorry for something the parent may be accusing you of doing, but it means that you are sorry that the parent feels so upset. It is a good way to diffuse some difficult situations. Here is an example:

"Mr. Johnson, I am so sorry that this is so upsetting. I have an idea about how it can be worked out. Why don't we sit down and brainstorm a list of alternatives?"

USE THE MIRROR RESPONSE

When you look into a mirror, your reflection does what you do. When you smile, so too does your reflection. When you move your arm, so too does your reflection. When you are with another person and you both are in harmony, both of you have similar body language just like your reflection. It is something that naturally occurs. When you sit opposite a friend in a restaurant and you both are in a friendly conversation, your body language is similar. When one person is talking and bending forward, the other person leans forward also. When two people are not in harmony, their body language does not match. Joel and Kathy were newly married. Kathy was upset with Joel because he refused to hang up his clothes. They were scattered across their apartment. Both of them were sitting opposite each other eating dinner. Joel stopped eating and had his arms folded across his chest. Kathy was leaning forward telling him why he should hang up his clothes. He had a frown on his face. She was wearing an artificial smile. Their body language was not at all similar. Instead, it reflected the differences of opinion they both had about this issue.

When you use the mirror response, you deliberately match some of your body language to the body language of the other person. When the difficult person leans forward, you lean forward matching the body movements. The only thing you keep different is your facial expression. Your facial expression needs to be calm.

STAND

If you want to keep a meeting short, stand while talking to the parent. It is uncomfortable to keep standing while talking. Parents will automatically shorten what they want to say, and the situation can be more easily diffused.

HOW TO HANDLE ANGRY PARENTS

Almost every teacher has had to face an angry parent (Winn Tutwiler, 2005). There are many reasons parents may become angry. Sometimes they become angry because of lack of communication. They find out from their child that some major change was made in their child's schedule or learning, and they have not been told.

Some parents become angry because they feel unimportant. They may have called the school, and no one returned their calls. They may also feel unimportant when they do get to talk to someone, and the person uses educational jargon that they do not understand. This can be embarrassing and confusing for parents. They are too embarrassed to admit they have no idea what the teacher is talking about, and they get angry because they want the conversation on their level. They feel disrespect from teachers whether it is true or untrue and that they have no control (Winn Tutwiler, 2005).

Some parents seem to walk around with chips on their shoulders. Just like some students are more prone to anger, some parents are also easily irritated. You just never know what will make them angry. Kahlia's mother was one of those mothers. She called the school constantly to complain about things that she felt were wrong. She didn't like the hours of the school day and wanted them to be changed. She wanted Kahlia to be able to wear skimpy halter tops and short shorts to school. She wanted water coolers in the classrooms and students to be allowed to use teachers' restrooms. Every day, it seemed there was something else that she wanted. The sad thing is that she complained so often that it was like the story of the boy who cried wolf. If she had a real complaint, everyone might have thought it was another one that was just impossible to resolve.

Kahlia's mother was unusual. Most parents get angry for a reason, and the anger grows and grows and grows until the parent explodes. It's important to nip anger in the bud before it escalates.

It took me many years both as a teacher and as an administrator to come up with a plan for angry parents. Before I had this plan, I floundered.

Sometimes, I gave in to the angry parent just to get them off my back. Other times, I reacted. Sometimes, I just tried to ignore it, but I soon learned that this didn't work as it just escalated and even spread to other parents. I took many classes on how to work with parents who were angry and hostile, and I tried new strategies that were unsuccessful. I finally found my own strategy that I am going to share with you now. It works for angry parents as well as many other hard-to-handle situations and parents.

THE NINE-STEP INTERVENTION

1. Set a Time to Meet

It has been my experience that when parents are upset, they want to talk to you right then and there. They may burst into the classroom while the teacher is teaching or even try to burst into an administrator's office. They have an issue, and they want it handled immediately.

This is the worst time to talk to them. Even if you were not busy, it would just be too difficult to talk while emotions are intense. The parent may not be the only one to say something that can be unreasonable. You may say something too that you later regret.

Set a time to meet later. This is very important. There is a four-point method for doing this:

1. Acknowledge the situation

2. Stay firm about rescheduling

3. Offer choices about rescheduling the new time

4. Stay positive

Cody's mother, Mrs. Hodges, was very angry and upset. She burst into the classroom and wanted to speak to his teacher, Mrs. Peterson, right away. Mrs. Peterson paused with what she was doing and turned to Mrs. Hodges.

Mrs. Hodges:	*I have to talk to you right now!*
Mrs. Peterson:	*I can see that you are upset. I will be glad to talk to you. I cannot speak right now, but I can talk to you later this afternoon when I am finished teaching.*
Mrs. Hodges:	*No! That won't work! It has to be right now.*
Mrs. Peterson:	*I'm so sorry to see you this upset. I will be glad to talk to you later. I can talk to you this afternoon at 3:30 or tomorrow morning at 7:30 or tomorrow afternoon at 3:30? Which one of those times works best for you?*

Mrs. Hodges: *I really want to talk to you now.*

Mrs. Peterson: *Yes, I can see that, and I am sorry I can't talk to you right now. Which time will work for you so we can meet and talk, today at 3:30, tomorrow morning at 7:30 or tomorrow afternoon at 3:30?*

Mrs. Hodges: *I suppose that today at 3:30 will work.*

Mrs. Peterson: *Great. I will see you at 3:30, Mrs. Hodges.*

Mrs. Peterson used the four points. She was patient. She acknowledged the problem, yet she stayed firm that she could not meet with Mrs. Hodges at that moment. She offered Mrs. Hodges choices. The choices empower the other person and also help to diffuse the situation at the time.

2. Make the Parent Feel Comfortable

When parents become angry, it is often because they are extremely anxious about something having to do with their child. It is important to make the parent feel comfortable so that it is a more productive visit. There are three points to helping parents feel more comfortable that help set the tone for a positive meeting.

1. Make the parent feel welcome

2. Have comfortable seating

3. Offer the parent something to eat or drink

Mrs. Peterson: *I'm so glad you could come back to meet at this time. (Smiles at parent.)*

Mrs. Hodges: *Thank you.*

Mrs. Peterson: *How about taking a seat here, and we will get started.*

Mrs. Hodges: *(Takes seat.)*

Mrs. Peterson: *I have some warm water here for coffee or tea and also some chocolates. Would you like some?*

Mrs. Hodges: *No, thank you.*

Mrs. Peterson set the tone by being warm and welcoming. She had prepared seating and even a snack for Mrs. Hodges. All of these contribute to diffusing anger and setting the scene to be calm.

3. Set a Mutually Agreed-Upon Goal

Begin the meeting by setting a positive goal for the meeting. This is very important because it ensures that both of you want the same outcome for the child. It identifies something that both you and the parent have in common (Wherry, 2008).

Mrs. Peterson: *I would like to set a goal for this meeting today, and that by time you leave, we have a plan for Cody, and we are both happy with the plan. Is that okay with you?*

Mrs. Hodges: *Yes, that sounds fine.*

When you set a goal, it shows that you and the parent agree on an outcome you both want. It automatically sets you both up as teammates working toward a common goal. Best of all, it helps to diffuse angry feelings because parents can see that you want the same outcome for their children.

4. Set a Time Boundary

Some parents will talk and talk and talk. It is important to set a boundary at the beginning of the meeting so that the parent knows how long you are available to talk. I like to have a small clock on the table as a reminder of the passing time.

Mrs. Peterson: *My tutoring class begins in forty minutes, so I can devote the next thirty minutes to you. I hope that is all right. I will keep track and tell you when we have ten minutes left.*

Mrs. Hodges: *(Nods head that it is OK.)*

5. Listen

Listening is a critical component. Many people know how to talk, but few know how to really listen. I have developed a process for listening that I call power listening. It is so important that I am devoting an entire chapter to it later in this book. For now, it is important to know four key components you need to use.

1. Take notes
2. Listen without interrupting
3. Nod your head
4. Summarize what you have heard

Invite the parent to tell you the problem. While the parent is speaking, take notes. There is something about taking notes that makes it more official for parents. It helps parents be more cautious about their words so that they do not become threatening or use bad language. Explain that you are taking notes so that you do not miss anything that is important.

While you are listening, do not interrupt. Instead, put your full attention on the parent nodding your head occasionally. This shows them that you are completely attentive and attuned to what you are hearing. Some of the things you may hear may be outrageous, but keep listening.

Mrs. Peterson: I am interested in hearing what you want to say.

Mrs. Hodges: (Talks.)

Mrs. Peterson: Let me see if I got this right. It sounded like you are very concerned about homework. You don't want Cody to have to do his homework because it cuts into his free time. Is that right?

Mrs. Hodges: Yes, that is right. He has no time to watch TV in the evenings because he has so much homework. He needs that time to relax and unwind.

It is very important to keep a straight face when you are listening to parents. I have had parents tell me their children need to come to school after class has started so they can sleep longer in the mornings. I just listen nodding my head putting my full attention on them.

Keep in mind that parents really want to be valued and they want to believe that you care about their children. When you use power listening, they feel empowered. Just talking about the problem helps.

6. Talk About Solutions

Now that you have listened to the parent, it's time to start talking about solutions to the problem. Instead of telling the parent "no" about an unreasonable request, find creative ways to tackle the problem. Offer parents choices in solving the problem. The more they are involved, the more they will be invested in ensuring the solution works.

Mrs. Peterson: OK, let's see what we can do about this. We'll tackle them point by point. (Point to your handwritten notes.) It sounds like Cody's homework is interfering with his time to watch television. I have to give him the same homework as I give the other students, but I do think I may have some ideas *to help this situation. Let's see which of these options you might like best. Cody has free time every afternoon after he has completed his work in class. That would be a great time to do most of his homework. I have other students who do that, and it seems to work well for them. Another idea is that Cody could get up earlier in the mornings and do his homework. Which of these options do you like, or do you have another idea of a way for him to do his homework without it interfering with his TV time?*

Notice how Mrs. Peterson did not tell Mrs. Hodges "no" at any point. She did set a clear boundary that Cody had to do his homework, yet she also offered options so that Mrs. Hodges could feel involved in creating a solution.

7. Listen and Finalize Plan of Action

After you have presented some options, use your power-listening skills as you carefully hear what the parent has said. You can repeat the process again if needed in which you once again present options. Together, come up with a plan of action for the problem.

Mrs. Peterson: *It sounds like you think it would work best for Cody to do his homework after he finishes his assignments in class. That sounds like we have a plan. How do you think we should handle telling Cody?*

Mrs. Hodges: *I will tell him at home, and then you can follow up at school.*

Mrs. Peterson: *That sounds like a great plan. When would you like to start?*

Mrs. Hodges: *Let's start tomorrow.*

Mrs. Peterson: *Great.*

8. Agree to Talk Again to Evaluate

A plan is only as good as its implementation. Therefore, it is important to set a time to talk again, either in person or on the phone, to discuss the plan's effectiveness.

Mrs. Peterson: *It sounds like we have a great plan. How about if we talk again in a week? We can see at that time if we have to make any adjustments. Does that work for you?*

Mrs. Hodges: *That sounds good.*

Mrs. Peterson: *How about if I call you one week from today at 3:30?*

Mrs. Hodges: *OK, here's my cell phone number.*

9. End in a Pleasant Way

Even after parents have found resolution, some may dawdle and want to talk some more. Take charge of ending the meeting and do it in a way that is pleasant and caring.

Mrs. Peterson: *I'm glad we talked about this and came up with a solution that will work best for Cody. Thank you for coming in. I will talk to you next week.*

Now that you know these nine steps, you are better equipped to handle angry parents as well as other hard-to-handle situations. I have used them many times, and they have always been effective for me. They do take lots of practice. Read them and the examples many times so that you learn them well. Print out the nine steps and have it located in a place that you can easily find if you need to review them in a hurry.

There is one more thing that is important to mention before moving on to the next chapter for handling other hard-to-handle situations, and that is there are some parents who are not only angry, but dangerous too. It is important if you think you may be dealing with a parent like this that you take steps to ensure that you are never alone with that parent. Have another faculty member present or arrange to meet the parent in a room that is part of the office where other faculty members are nearby if you need them.

Figure 3.1

The Nine-Step Intervention for Handling Angry Parents

Step 1: Set a time to meet

Step 2: Make the parent feel comfortable

Step 3: Set a mutually agreed-upon goal

Step 4: Set a time boundary

Step 5: Listen

Step 6: Talk about solutions

Step 7: Listen and finalize plan of action

Step 8: Agree to talk again to evaluate

Step 9: End in a pleasant way

How to Handle Parents With Bad Attitudes

4

A spoonful of words correctly phrased, helps communication be heard.

—Maryln Appelbaum

Parents of young children often sweeten medicine so their children will take it. The children would not have taken the medicine without the sweetener. Just as sweetening medicine can help medicine to be swallowed more easily, so too can using the right words help your message be heard. In this chapter, you will be learning specific tools for different types of hard-to-handle parents through communicating with them in a way that your message will be heard.

HOW TO HANDLE THE "KNOW-IT-ALL"

Know-it-all parents act like they are experts at everything (Bramson, 1981). The problem is they often think they know more than you and try to tell you how to do your job. There are effective strategies for handling these parents.

Acknowledge Their Knowledge

Underneath the veneer of the know-it-all is generally a person who needs to be respected and admired (Bramson, 1981). They want to feel that they are important, and that is why they show you and everyone else how much they know. Some of them actually do have a lot of knowledge.

47

Acknowledge the information that the parent does have (Capek Tingley, 2006.) They are not the true experts in teaching, you are! However, it helps parents to feel important and that their voice is heard when you acknowledge them.

"Mrs. Jones, you do know a lot. I am so glad that you are here today. We can combine our knowledge and skills to come up with a plan for Jamita."

Be Prepared

Make sure you have all the information that you need about the topics you will be addressing (Brinkman & Kirschner, 2002). If you feel the parent knows more than you, it can be intimidating. Be armed with facts about the topic of conversation (Politis, 2004). For example, if the student has been misbehaving, have a chart that shows the times the student misbehaved and the misbehaviors (Appelbaum, 2009a). This will help you show parents the actual number of times and dates that misbehavior occurred (see Figure 4.1).

Listen

The know-it-all has strong opinions. It is important that you take time to listen. Sometimes, all the parent really wants is someone to listen (Whitaker & Fiore, 2001).

Jason's mom, Mrs. Kiley, had to meet with Jason's teacher for a conference. Mrs. Kiley is a teacher too. She teaches at a different school, and she feels like she really understands her son Jason. Mrs. Kiley is in the process of going through a divorce from Jason's stepfather. She still has problems with her first husband, Jason's dad, who refuses to pay child support and has disappeared. She started out by telling Jason's teacher all the things a teacher "should do," and as the teacher sat there and listened courteously, she talked on about her own life. At the conclusion of the meeting, Mrs. Kiley thanked Jason's teacher for listening. She did not insist on anything. She started out as a "know-it-all" but ended as a parent who was going through a tough time.

Thank Them for Sharing Information

After you have listened, thank them, and then move on to the important issues that need to be covered.

"Mr. Wright, thank you so much for sharing that information. I also have information to share with you. Between the two of us, we will be quite a team working together with your son."

Figure 4.1

Behavior Frequency Assessment

Name of student _____ Student ID _____

Observer(s) _____ Date _____

The behavior being monitored is _____

_____

Observer's Initials	1	2	3	4	5	6	7	8	9	10	Time of Assessment

Provide a Way to Preserve Dignity

Sometimes what the know-it-all is saying is just plain wrong. It's important that you are cautious about how you tell them that they are wrong. Give them a way out gracefully so they are not embarrassed.

"Thank you for offering your opinions. While we are not allowed to implement that particular one, I am really glad that you are here. Here are some strategies that we can implement. Which one do you think will work best for your daughter?"

THE "BLAMER"

There are some parents who blame teachers for the problems of their children because it may be easier to blame the teacher than to blame themselves. It's easier to say, "It's your fault," than to think, "It's my fault." You cannot say to a parent, "You're blaming me instead of yourself." That absolutely will not work. It will only serve to make the parent angrier and defensive. The "three-part diffuser" works well in these situations.

The Three-Part Diffuser:

Part 1. Sounds like . . .

Part 2. I'm sorry you feel . . .

Part 3. Let's start now to . . .

Begin by acknowledging the feelings of the parent. Then apologize for the way the parent feels. This is not the same as taking responsibility for something that happened. The truth is that you are sorry that the parent feels like this. The whole situation could have been avoided if the parent did not feel like this. End with a plan to work together as a team.

Part 1. It sounds like you feel that we made some mistakes.

Part 2. I am sorry you feel that way.

Part 3. Let's start now to work on a plan so that Juan can succeed.

THE DEFENSIVE PARENT

Parents who are defensive are in some ways similar to parents who are blamers. Defensive parents do not want to be at fault for anything that happened with their children either. However, defensive parents make excuses for everything their children do. They come up with reasons for everything to avert blame.

When you are working with defensive parents, place no blame anywhere. That would make the situation worse. Instead talk to the parent in a firm yet calm voice (McEwan, 2005). Be a master of serenity as you speak. Stay focused on becoming a team with the parent working on behalf of the student. Here's an example of a dialogue between a defensive parent and a teacher.

Parent: I am so busy starting my new business that I had no idea that Pedro was in trouble. I ask him over and over again how he is doing, and he never tells me.

Teacher: Mrs. Martinez, I know you work long hours, and it is often difficult to make sure that Pedro's work is completed. I had no idea you were trying to build a business too. Wow! Let's talk now about what we can do to ensure that Pedro succeeds.

THE "HELICOPTER" PARENT

Helicopter parents are parents who hover over their children (Capek Tingley, 2006). They are parents who are extremely protective and want to make sure that everything is just right for their children. They can drive teachers crazy with silly requests on behalf of their children. Emma's mom said that tests needed to be written differently for her daughter. Anson's dad asked the teacher to put in new lightbulbs that were "fresher." Caitlin's mom said that her daughter needed to turn in all papers that are due a day later so that she would never feel pressure. Jon's dad said that the classroom heater needed to be warmer so that Jon wouldn't catch a cold. These are parents who want to sweep away any possible problems their children may ever experience.

Even though their requests are sometimes unreasonable and unworkable, it's important to remember that these are parents who have their children's best interests at heart. In some cases, these requests are also extremely beneficial for their children (Hoover, 2008). These parents do want to be involved in contrast to parents who do not call or ever come to the school. Although there may be times you may wish that these parents did not call or come to school, the upside is that they want to help their children. This makes it easier for you to become a team with them.

Have Patience

Exercise patience. Ethan was one of Mr. Landson's students who had not one, but two helicopter parents. It seemed that every time Mr. Landson turned around the first weeks of school, one of them was at his door or on the phone. They wanted to know how Ethan was doing, whether he had made any friends, and if he appeared to be happy. At first Mr. Landson became upset and wished they would just leave him alone. Then he realized how much they cared and became more patient.

Stay Ahead of the Game

When you have parents who hover and drop in or call at any time, it can be totally distracting from the things you need to accomplish. Stay ahead of the game by telling them when *you* will be contacting them. That puts you back in charge of the situation. In the example above, Mr. Landon told Ethan's parents that he would contact them for the next two weeks on a daily basis after school. He said that he was too busy to talk during the day but would call them at 4:15 daily. He had them give him the best number to reach them. Each day, he gave them an update. Initially, they still tried to contact him during the day, but he told them that he was in the middle of something and would be glad to talk to them at 4:15 as scheduled. They stopped pestering him when they saw that he was sticking to the plan.

At the end of the two weeks, he told them he was becoming busier with things to do for all of his students and he would be contacting them every other day. He did this for two more weeks and then switched to once a week. He and the parents became a really good team during this time because of their continual contact, and it was easier for him to talk to them when he was in charge of the times.

THE "NEGATIVE CYNICAL" PARENT

Parents who are cynical are suspicious about your motives and are likely to be heard saying things like, "That will never work." They are generally bitter about past situations and negative about everything. They complain and whine. Negative behavior can be contagious. However, so too can positive behavior.

Showcase the positives

Build trust by showcasing the positives in your classroom and with your students (McEwan, 2005). Have a bulletin board filled with photos of students having fun while learning. Make sure to include the child of this parent. Talk about the milestones that their child has made.

Have Examples of Work

Parents who are negative sometimes refuse to see the truth. Have examples of student assignments ready to show to parents. When they see the schoolwork their children are doing, it helps them realize their children are doing well.

Invite Involvement

When parents are negative and say that nothing will work, ask them what would work. Be persistent about having them come up ideas with you that will be a plan of success for their children.

Stay Positive

Stay positive regardless of how negative the parent may seem. Do not let yourself get down to a negative level. It will affect your work, and it will affect the work of your students.

If the parent is extremely negative when talking, it will be helpful if you stay focused on something positive. For example, Kathy Wilburn was Logan's teacher. She was middle-aged and recently married. She had thought that she was never going to marry and was now very happy. While Logan's dad was being negative, Kathy eyed her wedding ring and thought briefly about her new husband. It was a quick reminder of something positive. She was still actively involved in listening, but she also had something that served as a reminder to stay positive.

THE "BACKSTABBER"

Backstabbers are often referred to as "two-faced." They say one thing to your face and another thing behind your back. They are out to get you, but they do it in a sneaky way.

Ginny learned about backstabbers the hard way. She had just opened up a small, private school in an exclusive neighborhood. She was very excited about her school. She owned another larger private school in a different part of town that also kept her busy. The year the new school opened, she got someone to help her with the older school so that she could spend her days at the new school. Everything went well until the second year. Ginny hired one of the parents of a student to work at the new school as a teacher. Ginny no longer had someone to help her at the first school, so her time was much more split, and she was not at the newer school very much. When she went to the newer school, she thought everything was going great. The new parent–teacher told her that everything was fine. She always had a big smile on her face when she saw Ginny. It came as a total shock to Ginny that this parent–teacher had combined forces with another teacher, and they were going to open their own school. They had contacted all of the parents at Ginny's school, told them it was not a good school, and urged them all to go with them to the new school. Many did, and Ginny had to start over. She had been backstabbed!

Don't Turn Your Back

You will notice in the story about Ginny that she did not spend much time at the newer school. The backstabber took advantage of the fact that Ginny was not there. Stay ahead of the game by not turning your back! Stay current and focused on everything happening. Backstabbers do their best "stabbing" when you are not aware of it.

Bring the Information Forward

If you discover that someone is backstabbing you, gather information and confront the person. Take the sneakiness and bring it forth into the light of day. Backstabbers do things behind your back and are frequently at a loss when confronted. State the facts in a calm and matter-of-fact voice, and then wait for a response (Appelbaum, 1995b). If the person denies the situation, get out documentation that is evidence of the facts.

Do not ask the person why he or she did it. Do not get argumentative. This is not a time to get into a battle. Instead it's a time to bring forth the issues and get them resolved.

Set Boundaries and Follow Through

The backstabber may agree to your face to an issue but later try to find a way to backstab again. It is important to set boundaries so that this does not happen. Follow through by not turning your back on this person to ensure that the agreed behavior does indeed occur.

"Mrs. Brown, I understand that you want some changes made in the schedule. If you have recommendations, I would appreciate you telling me those recommendations. I will be sending out an e-mail to all of the parents about the procedure for making recommendations."

THE PARENT WHOSE CHILD "DOES NO WRONG"

Nearly everyone who has been in education has had parents who totally deny their children ever did anything wrong. When you hear them speak, you can almost see the little halos their little angels are wearing. It doesn't matter that the child is constantly in trouble because, for this parent, it just is not happening. It is impossible to work together as a team while the parent is in denial. You need strategies for success.

"He Never Does That at Home"

The parent who denies everything will often resort to saying, "My child never does that at home." You really can't know what the child does at home. The parent may be lying or denying the behavior. Here is an effective response to use:

"I am glad to hear that. If he did do it at home, what would you do?"

"My Child Didn't Do It"

Mr. Hayes was an elementary school teacher. He had been suspecting for awhile that one of his students, Aiden, was sneaking things out of his desk. As a test, he brought to school a leaky fountain pen and put it in his desk drawer, the drawer that was always missing items. Later that day he saw that his pen was missing. At the same time, he noticed that Aiden had blue ink all over one of his hands, his shirt, and his pants. Mr. Hayes decided that this was serious enough to warrant telling Aiden's parents. Aiden's mother came rushing over to the school extremely upset that her son might be in trouble. She saw her son and the stains all over his clothes and his hand, looked at Mr. Hayes, and said, "Aiden didn't do it." You need to have a positive response that still holds the child responsible.

"I cannot be positive he did. The evidence (pointing to evidence) looks like he did do it. In case, he did do it, how do you think we can handle it?"

"My Child Never Lies to Us"

When students get into trouble and think that their parents will be contacted, they may go home and tell their parents what occurred with a twist to make themselves look innocent. When parents are contacted, they take the child's side and say, "My child never lies to me." They want to believe this is true so much that otherwise reasonable parents believe their child (Whitaker & Fiore, 2001).

In my work as a therapist, I have worked with families of addicts. Many of these families want to believe so much in their children that over and over again they believe stories that their addicted family members tell them. This can go on for years and years. It's tough to acknowledge that a family member is an addict. The same dynamics occur in families of children who get in trouble at school. Parents want to believe their children are truthful, so they will frequently accept their word over the word of the teacher. It's important to be very tactful with these family members. You cannot come in like a bulldozer and say, "It's simply not true. Your child is a liar." They will turn their backs on you, and you will not be able to work together as a team.

Defining the Lie

Many years ago I worked in a clinic with problem teens. One of my clients, who I will call Ben, came in weekly to meet with me. He told me some pretty wild stories of things that were happening in his life. I soon realized that the stories were untrue. I was still young and in training, and I discussed Ben with a supervising psychologist. I still remember what this psychologist told me. He said that one of the reasons that people lie is to protect themselves. I thought about Ben and some of his responses to me when I asked him questions, and I realized that this was very true with Ben. Since that time, I have seen this happen over and over again with children. They say, "I didn't do it," when the evidence is very visible. They lie to protect themselves so they won't get into trouble.

When parents tell you that their children never lie, it may be true that in the past their children didn't lie. You cannot know this for sure because you were not there. You do know, however, that now their child is in trouble and lying.

Present the Evidence

Be prepared when you meet with parents. Have the proof with you so that there is something visible for parents to see. Have copies of homework and classwork so parents can see for themselves the work their children are doing.

Create a behavior notebook using a three ring binder. Divide the binder with page separators that have tabs. Have student names in alphabetical order on the tabs. When students misbehave, they record their own specific inappropriate behavior. They sign and date it, and it is placed inside the Behavior Notebook. If students cannot write, you write what they dictate and then read it back.

The behavior notebook is a great tool for preventing lies to parents and for clearly showing parents that their children did engage in misbehavior. It is difficult for students to lie to their parents after they have signed their names on a sheet of paper describing their own misbehavior. It is even more difficult for parents to continue to believe their children when they see their children's signature on the behavior sheet (see Figure 4.2).

Figure 4.2

My Behavior

Student's name _____

Date _____ Time of day _____

Teacher _____

My inappropriate behavior was _____

_____

_____

_____

_____

_____

_____

_____

_____

_____

I learned from this _____

_____

_____

_____

_____

_____

_____

_____

_____

_____

_____

_____

Student's signature _____

Be Tactful

Be very careful when speaking to parents. Here is an example of an approach that is tactful yet also acknowledges the truth of what occurred.

"Mrs. Jennings, it sounds like you have a special relationship with your child in which your child has a history of telling you the truth. That is great! Here is what I saw yesterday in our classroom. (Describe what occurred and show evidence.) I have some ideas on how to handle it, but I would like to know your ideas too. Together, we can come up with a plan so that your child experiences great success."

THE PARENT WHO THINKS YOU ARE NOT FAIR

There are parents who use the words, "You're not fair," just to get what they want. Nothing you do for them is ever enough. Ironically, I have heard their children use those same words in the classroom telling teachers, "You're not fair."

Make Sure You Are Fair

First and foremost, be sure to be fair (Whitaker & Fiore, 2001). Students can sense when you are not being fair, and that makes you fair game for them to tell their parents. You may have favorites to whom you are unconsciously giving extra consideration. Rethink how you manage your classroom and the students so that you do it fairly. Think over your actions. Was it possible to misinterpret something you said or did? It's important that students feel they are cared about, and that no one student is cared for more than another student (Houston & Bettencourt, 1999).

Fair Is Not Equal

While you need to care for all your students, it's important to know that treating students fairly is not always equal. Here's a story to illustrate this concept. Dr. Jones is a dentist who treats many patients each day. Three people come to his office one morning all at the same time. The first one has a horrible toothache. The second one had a crown fall off of a tooth so that there is just a tiny stub where the tooth was. The third patient is there for a regular checkup. Dr. Jones sees all three patients and wants to treat them equally, so he decides to pull a tooth from the mouth of each person. They were all treated equally, but was he being fair? Each patient had his or her own special needs. To be fair, each of those needs should be treated differently. It is the same with students. They too each are different and unique. There are times when you can treat them all equally, but there are other times when it is not fair to individual students to do this. Some students need extra time on assignments. Some students work better alone than in small groups. Some students learn best visually while others learn best in an auditory or tactile manner. Every student is different, and every student needs to be treated fairly.

When you are speaking to parents who think you may not be fair to their child, you can give them the analogy of the dentist and his three patients to help them understand that each child is different. Each child is unique and needs help to reflect his or her individual needs. That is being fair. That is treating all children in ways that helps each child succeed.

"Mrs. Coulter, I appreciate how you feel about Gavin. Each of my students is so special and so is Gavin. I will do my best to help him learn. Your suggestions are always welcome, and when they can be accommodated, I will do them."

THE PARENT WHO IS EXTREMELY ANGRY

In the previous chapter, you learned the nine-step intervention for angry parents. Some parents are not only angry but also hostile. It is very difficult to talk to parents who are extremely angry and hostile (Bender, 2005). They are not thinking clearly and neither are you. It is difficult to think clearly when someone is "in your face" attacking you. You need some strategies that will help both you and the parent.

Anger and hostility are secondary emotions

Anger and hostility are different from emotions like love and fear. When you feel love or fear, it is often instantaneous. They are primary emotions. Anger is not a primary emotion. It is a secondary emotion (Appelbaum, 2009a). Think about the last time that you got very angry. Picture the situation. Picture the people involved. Think about what you were feeling before you felt the anger. My guess is that you were first feeling worry, fear, hurt, guilt, or frustration. When parents are angry at you, they may first have primary emotions such as the ones I have just mentioned.

It is often easier to handle parents who are angry when you realize this. These may very well be parents who care so much for their children that they are hurting inside at the thought of anything being wrong. It is often easier for some people to express anger than to express the other primary emotions. Emmanuel's mother, Mrs. Garcia, was very angry.

Emmanuel had just received his report card and was failing two of his subjects and doing poorly in the others. She took out her anger on Ms. Lindsey, Emmanuel's teacher. However, the truth was that she felt very guilty and frustrated. Her employer had demanded that she work overtime for the past six weeks. That left her with very little time to spend with Emmanuel. She felt she had failed him as a parent.

Act, Instead of React

It's important that you don't react to the anger and hostility (Sanderson, 2005). Instead take time to become calm, think clearly, and then make a choice. While you cannot control how the other person is feeling, you can control how you are feeling. It is your decision on how you will respond. Stay objective (Bender, 2005). Keep the facts clearly in front of you. The other person is angry. You have choices in your response.

Use the Nine-Step Approach

If appropriate, use the steps you learned in Chapter 3 for handling angry and hard-to-handle people and situations.

Move to a Private Area

If the parent is making a scene, it can be frightening to students. Guide the parent gently and firmly to a more private area. There are several ways you can do this. One way is to request that the parent goes with you somewhere else. "Mrs. Wilson, let's go to my classroom now so we can talk about this." Start moving in that direction as you make the request.

If you see that the parent is too irrational for you to make a request, simply start moving away saying, "I'm moving into my classroom so we can talk." You are just stating the facts as you say this. They will generally start following you.

If you are frightened by the parent's behavior, start walking to the office as you talk to the parent. This happened to Lori Tiles. She was a petite, quiet, first-year teacher. She took one look at Mr. Preston, a six-foot angry and hostile father, who was pointing his finger at her as he shouted, and she knew that she needed help. She very quietly said as she walked toward the office, "I can see that you are really upset, Mr. Preston. Let's get you some resolution in our office. I'm heading that way, so we can talk there. Together, we will get this handled." Mr. Preston kept talking and shouting, but he walked along with Lori to the office.

Use the Detach-With-Empathy Approach

Stay calm and collected. Detach from taking what the hard-to-handle parent is saying personally. Remember that sometimes it is not about you. It may be about the parent's own feelings of guilt, frustration, or just the way the person is wired to handle situations. Stay empathetic and caring while not letting yourself become overwhelmed by the parent.

Stay Safe

I mentioned in Chapter 3 the importance of being safe. There are some parents that you may always meet with in more public places. Trust your instincts. It is better to be safe than sorry. Talk to your principal or another administrator if you are frightened by a parent's behavior.

Listening Skills for 5 Hard-to-Handle Parents

Sticks and stones can break bones, but painful words can break the spirit.

—Maryln Appelbaum

You may be wondering why there is a chapter on how to listen in a book on how to handle hard-to-handle parents. It is because listening skills are an important component of communication, and effective communication is an important key to building relationships between educators and parents (Lasky, 2000). The strategies in this book will work not only with hard-to-handle parents but also with parents who are more passive and speak very little.

This chapter begins with an explanation of communication and then teaches the art of listening. I believe that listening is an "art." Just like an artist paints a painting, the effective listener also creates a painting. In art, the artist starts with a blank canvas, and soon, it is filled with something that is special and meaningful to the artist and to those who see the artwork. The effective listener starts with a blank canvas too. When using effective listening skills, the canvas is filled with all of the different colors that are revealed as the parent talks. The colors are the parent's feelings and desires. The artist puts all those colors together onto the canvas of life, and together, the educator and the parent complete a canvas that is unique and special to help the student. Best of all, as the canvas is created, a special bond forms between the artful listener and the parent so the result is a canvas of teamwork on behalf of the child.

THE COMMUNICATION PROCESS

Many people think that communicating is about talking, but in reality there is so much more to communication than just talking. The words, themselves, only represent seven percent of communication (Decker, 1988). Body language and facial expression represent fifty-five percent of communication. They, in fact, tell others more than words do! When people nod their heads, stamp their feet, smile, or put out a hand in greeting, those are all forms of communication that are powerful. All of these impact the way words are said. For example, if a person says the word "please" and looks up begging, there would be one response. If another person says the word "please" with a sneer on his face, there would be another response. The body language and facial expression said more than the actual word.

Another key component of communication is the tone of voice used when words are spoken (Decker, 1988). The tone and emphasis used when speaking can completely change the meaning of words. For example, the same word, "please," will have different meanings if it is said with impatience, if it is whispered, or if it is shouted. The tone and emphasis is called the vocal part of communication and is thirty-eight percent of communication.

It's important to know this because when you listen to parents, pay attention to more than their words.

POWER LISTENING

Power listening is a powerful method of listening. It is a way of listening that shows the other person that you care and that you want to hear what he or she has to say.

Most conversation is superficial. This is common. When you go to the grocery store, you do not need to have a deep conversation with the person who checks you out at the cash register. When you go to the restaurant, you do not need to have a deep conversation with the waiter or waitress. However, when you are handling hard-to-handle parents, you do need to connect and be able to communicate. That is when you will need to use power listening.

Here's how it works. The speaker has a message that is a combination of words and feelings. The speaker puts together the message, the words, and states them in words, tone, facial expression, and body language to the listener (see Figure 5.1).

Figure 5.1 The Listening Process

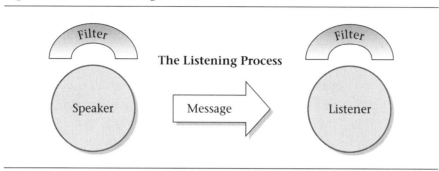

The listener hears and sees the person speaking. The listener has filters that sift through everything that is being said (Gordon, 2000). Those filters include prejudices, facts, opinions, and past experiences. The filter can become a barrier to understanding what the speaker is saying. For example, the listener may be a teacher who has listened to the parent many times in the past for hours and hours. When the parent starts speaking, the filter within the teacher–listener may say, "Here we go again," and tune out what the parent is saying. For power listening to occur, those barriers must be broken down. The listener then can hear what the speaker says.

Interestingly, the speaker also has a filter. It too is composed of all of the speaker's prejudices, facts, opinions, and past experiences. For example, Miss Thompson was Cole's mother. Cole is a child with ADHD and Autism Spectrum Disorder. She had had problems in the past with his teachers not understanding Cole. When Miss Thompson came to Cole's conference with his third grade teacher, she brought her filters along. While Cole's teacher talked, Miss Thompson was thinking, "She won't care about him any more than his other teachers have." When she tried to tell the current teacher that she wanted her to help her son, she expressed all of the impatience that she had felt over the last three years with other teachers.

Power listening helps break through these barriers, these filters, so that true communication and teamwork can occur.

Door Openers

Door openers open the doors to communication (Gordon, 2000). They allow the listener to listen in an empathetic manner that respects the other person (McNaughton, Hamlin, McCarthy, Head-Reeves, & Schreiner, 2007). Following are several easy and effective door openers.

"Really . . ."

"Ummm . . ."

"Sounds like . . ."

When you are listening, occasionally make a sound such as "ummm" or say a word such as "really" to show the parent that you are listening attentively. Use "sounds like" to summarize the feeling that the parent is conveying. For example, Kendra's mom was talking to Mrs. Jacobs, Kendra's teacher. She was telling her that Kendra's behavior had totally changed. She said that Kendra was not eating as well and was having trouble falling asleep. She said that when Kendra did fall asleep, she was having nightmares and would wake up screaming. Mrs. Jacobs listened to her, occasionally saying, "Really" or "Ummm." She added, "Sounds like these changes are frightening." Kendra's mom nodded her head and said, "Yes, it sure is," and then went on talking some more.

More Door Openers

"Tell me about it."

"Would you like to talk about it?"

"What do you think about it?"

"I would really like to hear more about it."

All of these door openers open the doors to communication by expressing concern and interest in what the parent has to say (Appelbaum, 1995a).

Body Language

Your body language is another very important factor in communication. The way you sit, your facial expression, attentiveness, and gestures all show you care. A key factor in body language is showing that you are attentive. When I teach power listening at a seminar, I like to do an exercise that demonstrates the power of being attentive. Each audience member gets a partner, and they decide who will be A and who will be B. They each think about their most difficult parent. The person who is designated as A starts talking first describing the difficult parent while B listens. Just prior to the exercise starting, the B's are told to look at their watch, look at the door, and look at others in the room while the A's are speaking. Afterward, they are asked how that felt. The A's always say, "It was horrible." The point is made that when listening, it is important to put your entire attention on the speaker. It is disruptive to look other places while listening. When you are attentive, your body language shows that you care.

Eye contact is an important factor in body language. Be careful with different cultures (Jaksec, 2003). In the United States, it is generally considered appropriate to have eye contact to the point that when people avoid eye contact, people think of the person as avoiding them. While this is the case in the United States, the opposite may actually be true for some other cultures. There are cultures in which direct eye contact is considered offensive and intrusive. It is often better when you are in doubt of cultural sensitivity to sit side by side so that eye contact will be minimized rather than face the parent. Be cautious also when speaking to a parent who is a different gender. Too much eye contact can be misconstrued as being seductive. That is something you never want to happen when you are striving to build a professional relationship with a parent.

While you are listening, occasionally nod your head up and down to indicate you are hearing and understanding what the parent is saying. It shows the person you are paying attention.

Uncross your arms. Crossed arms frequently indicate being closed off. When your arms are open, you are showing the parent that you are open and receptive to what the parent is saying.

Make sure your facial features indicate that you are paying attention to what the parent has to say. Your face is like a reflection in a mirror. It reflects everything you are feeling. If you are going to speak to a parent who is hard to handle, take time to compose yourself. Think of the student. Think of how important it is for you to be a team. Keep yourself focused on this instead of feeling dislike for the parent. If you allow yourself to feel dislike and disrespect, it will show up in your face, and instead of your face being a door opener to better communication, it will be a door closer.

A Word of Caution

There are some forms of body language that show disinterest, and you may not even realize that you are using them. Avoid tapping a pencil, tapping your foot, or slouching in your chair. All of your mannerisms need to reflect your concern and interest.

Physical Space

I remember watching a comedy episode in which there was a close talker. The people in the episode made it a big spoof whenever this person stood really close. I personally have had similar experiences on rare occasions where someone gets too close to me, and I find myself backing away and also not listening as well. When you are planning the meeting, take time to think about the physical space between you and the parent. If you sit opposite each other, sit approximately three feet or four feet apart. If you sit closer, it's too close. If you sit farther apart, it's sometimes too far. If you are sitting side by side, sit close enough that you can show the parent any student work or documentation, but not so close that you could accidentally have your leg or hip or arms touching.

ONCE THE DOOR HAS BEEN OPENED

It's great to use door openers throughout the conversation because they keep the parent talking. There are other things that you can do too to help parents clarify what they are saying.

Summarize

Occasionally summarize what you have heard.

"It sounds like you are saying that Corrine does not sleep well at night, and you think that may be causing problems with her school work. Did I get that right?"

Restate Key Words

When the parent pauses, it is sometimes helpful to restate a key word that the parent has said. This helps the parent stay on track.

Parent: *I hate that Anthony gets in trouble all the time.*

Teacher: *Hate . .?*

Parent: *Yes, I hate it. It makes me feel like a failure as a parent.*

Avoid Door Closers

Just as there are door openers, there are also door closers. Door closers close the door to communication (Gordon, 2000). If you want to hear what the parent has to say, it's important to avoid these door closers.

- Interrupting
- Analyzing
- Giving your own example

Interrupting

Have you ever talked to someone and felt you could not get a word in? Every time you say something, that person interrupts and inserts his or her own wording. It quickly becomes a one-way conversation. You soon start to feel that this is a person in whom you cannot confide. Instead, it seems like the person always turns the conversation around and blocks you. Here's an example of interrupting as a door closer.

Parent: *My son never listens to me, and I get so . . .*

Teacher: *I know exactly what you mean. That happens in my class too.*

Notice how the parent did not get to finish the statement; that teacher will never know what the parent was going to say. It could have been that the parent was expressing frustration, but it also could have been that the parent was going to say he or she got so angry that severe punishment was meted out. It could even be that the parent is happy because it means her child is independent. All of these would directly impact how the student behaves in the classroom. Interrupting the speaker closed the doors to finding out more information.

Analyzing

People do not like to be analyzed. It is frightening to think that every word said will be weighed and picked apart.

Parent: *Jordan reminds me of my husband, the way he bullies.*

Teacher: *So your husband and your son bully others. Did one of your parents bully you too?*

The teacher in the above example carried it too far. People don't want to be analyzed when they come to school to discuss their child. It's delving too deeply and getting too personal. It does not create an atmosphere of trust and, instead, closes doors to communication.

Giving Your Own Example

This is an easy and common mistake. When one person speaks, the person listening is reminded of a similar problem. The listener tells the speaker details about the problem, and how it was resolved. This is a door closer. The solution that works for one parent will not necessarily work for another parent. Everyone is different. It is important to remember this while listening to parents talk. Providing your own example can shut the doors to communication because parents feel that their own answer would not be as correct.

Parent: *My daughter hits me every time she gets angry.*

Teacher: *I had that happen with my child. Here's what I did to handle it . . .*

In the example above, there may be more going on. The teacher needed to listen and find out more facts. Then if the teacher wanted to offer some suggestions, she could have instead given a list of suggestions and asked the parent which one would work better for her. That would have empowered the parent.

Remember the Tip of the Iceberg

The door closers just listed cut off parents from talking more. Therapists and counselors know that when a client comes to them with a problem, the real problem may be something deeper. The client starts with something that is easier to discuss. This is the "tip of the iceberg." Buried inside the iceberg is what is really bothering the person. If the therapist treats the surface problem, the real problem will be stuck deep within the iceberg. When a parent comes to you with a problem, sometimes it too is the tip of the iceberg. I have had angry parents who came in to talk to me about something they felt the school or I was doing wrong. When I sat and listened using the strategies you are learning in this chapter, it turned out to be something completely different that was bothering the parent. One parent started out very angry, and as I listened, her real story came out. Her husband had been diagnosed with Bipolar Disorder, and she was terrified that her child might have it too. Another parent came in to complain, and as I listened, I found out that there was domestic violence in her home. Still another told me that she had a terminal illness, and she had not told her child about it.

This is why it is critical to listen effectively and not jump in to try and solve a problem immediately. If you do, you may be solving the immediate problem, the tip of the iceberg, but not helping the parent find true resolution. Parents will come back over and over again if only the tip of the iceberg is addressed.

The best way to learn to listen is to practice, practice, and practice some more. When you finish listening, use the checklist in Figure 5.2 to see if you remembered to use the skills you have been learning.

Many years ago I wrote this poem that sums up listening skills. I gave it as a gift at my trainings. It is my gift to you now to sum up this chapter on listening. I call it "The Greatest Gift."

Figure 5.2

Listening Checklist			
	Yes	Maybe	No
Uses door openers			
Nods head			
Leans forward			
Uses effective eye contact			
Is totally attentive			
Restates key words			
Summarizes			
Uses appropriate facial expression indicating interest			
Maintains appropriate physical space while listening			
Omits personal situations and examples			
Avoids analyzing			
Avoids interrupting			
Has arms uncrossed			
Remembers tip of the iceberg			

THE GREATEST GIFT

The greatest gift of all

cannot be bought in stores or malls

It is the treasure of being heard

truly heard

It is the gift of listening to

hopes, fears, dreams, hurts

Listening demonstrates

acceptance, caring, and hope

Taking time to listen

fosters trust and respect

The gift of your presence

truly listening opens doors to caring relationships

It's the greatest gift of all.

How to Talk
so Parents Listen

6

Once a word has been spoken, it can never be taken back.

—Maryln Appelbaum

The skills you have learned in earlier chapters have been mostly in response to situations in which parents confronted you. They were the ones with problems. There are many times you are the one with a problem. When this happens, you need to know how to talk so parents will listen and respect what you say. This chapter will give you the skills you need to be the one to initiate tough conversations and get through to parents so they listen. You will learn the art of being persuasive and assertive. These are powerful skills that you can use not only with difficult parents but with all difficult hard-to-handle people that you may encounter in your life.

FIVE STYLES TO MANAGE FRUSTRATION AND ANGER

When people become upset and have a problem, there are five different ways that they generally use to cope. The first four methods are ineffective. The fifth one is effective. It is the one that you will be learning to use. It is a powerful way to get others to listen in a respectful manner.

1. Aggressive Style

People who become aggressive when they are upset will say and do anything without regard for the feelings of the other people involved. They realize they are hurting others and often actually intend to hurt others (Franzoi, 2000). While it is healthy to express feelings, it is not appropriate to express them without taking into consideration the feelings of others.

Words can and do hurt. Gossip and spreading bad or false rumors are also forms of aggression. They are indirect aggression (Franzoi, 2000). Words can be as painful in their own way as physical abuse. People more frequently remember negative things they have heard than positives. Negative hurtful words can replay themselves over and over again in the victim's mind and have a negative impact on self-esteem as well as other relationships.

When someone says, "Nice outfit," people frequently respond, "Thanks," and just go on with what they were saying. If anyone said, "Wow, that color does not look good on you," the person would have a much harsher reaction. Negative words are like tiny flames of disharmony that can rage into a huge forest fire.

People who are aggressive will bulldoze others to get what they want. They will say and do anything to get what they want without caring about the rights of others (Appelbaum, 1995b). They are more concerned about winning at any cost. There is a lack of respect for others. These are people who are not generally liked, and are sometimes feared. Here are some examples of aggressive statements.

"Do it or else."

"If you don't do it, there will be dire consequences."

"Get on it now!"

"What are you waiting for . . . spring to come?"

You can easily see that some of these statements are bossy, domineering, sarcastic, and even bullying (Drew, 2004). They all make the other person feel badly if they do not do what the aggressive person wants.

2. Passive–Passive Style

People who are totally passive are the opposite of those that are aggressive. Instead of asking for what they want, they hold everything in (Appelbaum, 1995b). They do what the other person wants. They frequently do not even consciously realize that they are angry. If the passive person does express his or her needs, it is done in an apologetic way, or it may be through dropping hints rather than coming out and saying what is needed. Here are some examples of passive statements. They are usually said in a meek or apologetic voice.

"Is it all right if we sit down?"

"I'm so sorry to ask you this."

"I was thinking we maybe could have a quick meeting sometime."

The passive person generally takes full responsibility for whatever is wrong. The person may become a caretaker trying to fix everyone else and make things right. This person eventually gets worn out trying to accommodate the needs of everyone else. For example, Miss Jennings was a first-year teacher in high school. Her students constantly took advantage of her, and she was constantly apologizing to them. When it came time for parent conferences, parents told her all the things they wanted her to do. She thought being a good teacher was doing what parents wanted. This was the way to have teamwork. Eventually, she got so worn out trying to please everyone that she decided teaching was just too hard and quit.

3. Passive–Explosive Style

People who are the passive–explosive type are different from the passive–passive type because they know they are angry, but they are afraid to do anything about it, so they hold it in and hold it in and hold it in, and then find themselves exploding over something that may be insignificant. For them, it was the straw that broke the camel's back!

When they explode, they say words that they often later regret.

"I am so sick of listening to you and doing what you want."

"I've listened to you long enough. I'm fed up."

Afterward, the person who exploded often feels guilty and sometimes feels the need to make amends asking forgiveness from the other person. The irony is that the other person may have been wrong in the first place, but now the person who exploded also feels wrong and winds up being the one to apologize

Instead of exploding outwardly, the person may explode inwardly. When this happens, the person turns all the anger toward himself or herself and may become depressed. This is a result of "in-pressing" (holding in) their feelings. "Why couldn't I stand up to that parent? Why didn't I say what I meant? Why do I hold everything in? I just never can stand up for myself." You can see that those negative thoughts are directed "in." They are in-pressing instead of expressing in an appropriate manner.

4. Passive–Aggressive Style

Another way to cope with anger is to be passively aggressive. Individuals who cope in a passive–aggressive style may frequently sulk and be resentful about what others want them to do. They may have deliberate forgetfulness and agree to do something and later say they forgot. They may also procrastinate doing something because they really do not want to do it and because they feel the demands are unreasonable (Appelbaum, 1995b). They do not express their anger openly, but instead do it in these other subtle, hidden ways.

People with this type of style do not stand up and ask for what they want. Instead, they do it in a passive–aggressive way. They are still violating the rights of others because they are not considering the feelings of others. People who use this style may deny there is a problem but then go and do whatever they want anyhow. They may find ways to sabotage others. Mrs. Crandall wanted to go on a vacation with her husband, Mr. Crandall. He wanted to go to Mexico. She wanted to go to Canada. She did not tell him that she did not want to go to Mexico. Instead, she told him stories nightly of people who had gone to Mexico and had had problems. She told him that several friends got ill from drinking the water. She told him that someone else had gotten lost and could not find help. She also left brochures lying around their home with information about Canada. When he still did not get her "hints," she became ill with a stomach bug and said that she could not risk going to Mexico and have it become worse.

You can see this same behavior in your students who take so long to do an assignment that it is time to move on to the next assignment. They really did not want to do it. You can also see it with parents who arrive late each time to conferences because they did not really want to come. The time set aside for the conference is nearly finished by the time they arrive. You can even see it in your own behavior when you feel overwhelmed by a parent's requests and agree to do something and then don't do it.

5. Assertive Style

People who are assertive stand up for what they want and need. They do it in a way that does not violate the rights of others (Appelbaum, 1995b). They feel good about asking for what they want even if they don't get it. They feel good because they *did* ask and because they did it in a respectful way. It is the best method for handling anger and frustration.

KEYS TO BEING ASSERTIVE

Define the Problem

Before you can begin to think of speaking to a parent about an issue, it's important to define the specific problem (Sanderson, 2005). You have to be very clear about the issues. It helps to write the details so they become even clearer. Write the approximate date the problem began and approximate dates for milestone events relating to the problem.

Write down sources that can validate there is a problem (Sanderson, 2005). Is the problem something you saw happen with your own eyes? Is it something that someone else has told you? If it is something that someone else told you, how reliable is that source? Sometimes, people will, for whatever reason, tell you a story about parents or other teachers that are untrue. If you confront individuals with a problem without verifying the truth of each story, you will be creating bigger problems. It is easy for gossip to start and spread like a wildfire getting wilder and wilder and more and more untrue.

When you are defining the problem, it's important to also think about the impact the problem has had on you and on individuals who are involved (Sanderson, 2005). Is it something that is extremely stressful? What will happen if you do not take action?

Turn the Problem Into an I-Statement

Once you have defined the problem, write a sentence about the problem. Keep it simple. Leave out your feelings and stick to the facts. Here are some examples:

Example 1: Mrs. Sanchez interrupts my class two or more times a week while I'm teaching.

Notice how clearly this is stated. It is not a statement that says, "I want to pull my hair out if I see her one more time at my door." It is not a statement that says, "This woman is a pain." Instead it is a simply worded statement of fact.

Example 2: Jordan needs parental support at home to complete his homework.

This too is clearly worded and leaves all emotions out of the statement. It does not say anything negative about Jordan's parents. It avoids putting any blame on the family or on Jordan.

POWER REQUEST

Once you have the statement, it is time to rephrase it so that it becomes a power request. The Power Request in Figure 6.1 has several components (Appelbaum, 1995b).

Figure 6.1

Components of the Power Request
Parent's Name
Power Pause
The Problem
Power Pause
Statement of Need

Parent's Name

Always start by saying the person's name (Dawson, 1992). People like to hear their own name. It is a sign of both respect and recognition.

Power Pause One

After you say the parent's name, pause for a second. This puts more emphasis on what you are going to say. It also shows the parent that you are not rushing. You have carefully prepared what you are going to say.

The Problem

Briefly describe the problem. It needs to be a short sentence. The longer it is, the more likely that it will get too complex. You may lose the parent's attention before you have even made your request. Make sure that you do not complain when you tell the problem. It is just a brief statement of facts.

Power Pause Two

After you have stated the problem, pause again. This once again gives emphasis to what you are saying and captures the attention of the parent.

Statement of Need

Ask for what you need. Be sure to use the words, "I need" or "I would appreciate" rather than "I want." It is easier for parents to hear and helps ensure they will honor your request.

It is important to use the first person when making the request, "I need." This is much more effective than saying, "You need." When you begin with "You need . . .," you are taking away the power of the other person. You are telling that person what to do rather than framing it as a request. People get mad when they are told what to do. Even if they agree with what you say, they may say "no" because of the sense of lack of control.

See Figure 6.2 for how the power request looks using the two examples given earlier.

Figure 6.2

Two Examples Using the Power Request

Example 1: Mrs. Sanchez interrupts the class two or more times a week while the teacher is teaching.

Parent's Name	*"Mrs. Sanchez"*
Power Pause One	Pause for emphasis
The Problem	*"My class gets distracted when there are interruptions."*
Power Pause Two	Pause for emphasis
Statement of Need	*"I would appreciate it if you'd call and make appointments before you come to the school."*

Example 2: Jordan needs parental support at home to complete his homework.

Parent's Name	*"Mr. Carter"*
Power Pause One	Pause for emphasis
The Problem	*"Jordan's overall grade could be higher if he turned his homework in."*
Power Pause Two	Pause for emphasis
Statement of Need	*"I would appreciate it if you'd create a special time daily for Jordan to do his homework."*

POWER PERSUASION

Now that you have the words to use, there are some other tools you need to know to help ensure success with hard-to-handle parents when you have a problem.

Think of Parents as VIPs

Actually parents are VIP's, very important people. They are very important people because they exert a powerful influence over their children's lives. Even when children act like they do not care what their parents think, they still do. They still want the approval and the attention of their parents.

I did some work for a period of time in a residential treatment program for children who had been severely abused, molested, or both. These cases were so severe that the children had to be removed from their homes. Their parents had to attend classes to demonstrate to the courts that they were really trying to get their children back. I remember one child who had been terribly abused. Her mother was an alcoholic who would beat her when she got into a drunken rage. She brought strange men into the house at all hours of the day or night. Sometimes, when she was passed out cold, the men would molest her daughter. This daughter still loved her mom and was extremely loyal to her. She wanted very much to go back and live with her. The point of this story is that children do care about their parents. They may get angry and rebellious, but almost all children still care just like this girl did for her mother.

Treat parents like very important people (Dawson, 1992). Be courteous and respectful in your greetings and when you speak to them. They will appreciate it, and it will go far in helping you ask them for their help.

Think Positive Thoughts as You Greet Parents

Mentally prepare yourself before each meeting with parents. Think of something positive about the parents. Nicole was a new teacher who thought she was really good at communication. When she met with parents to speak to them, she found that she had a lot to learn. Her facial expressions betrayed her true feelings toward parents. She knew she had to do something to mentally prepare herself so that this did not continue to happen. She spent time thinking about building a caring team. She thought about the hard work it is to be a parent. She psyched herself up. It worked. And that is what you have to do too. You have to psyche yourself up so that you greet parents warmly. Shake hands as you greet them, and think of something positive about them (Dawson, 1992). Parents can sense if you are smiling at them and are thinking something negative at the same time. Here's an example outside of the classroom.

Caroline, a secondary school teacher, walked into a clothing store to buy some new clothing. She had just cashed her paycheck and had some of the cash in her wallet. She had changed clothes and was wearing a pair of faded blue jeans, sneakers, and a big floppy shirt. She looked around the store and found some clothing she liked. She tried to get the salesperson to help her, but the clerk ignored her. She gathered up an armful of clothing and was going to go try them on, when suddenly her cell phone rang. She tried shifting the clothing in her arms as she reached for the phone, and her purse fell down, her wallet packed with cash fell on the floor. When the sales clerk looked down and saw the wallet filled with money, she came up to Caroline, and with a warm smile, now said, "Can I help you?" This same sales clerk ignored her until her wallet fell out. Caroline looked at the sales clerk and could not help but think, "I am being manipulated." It is the same with parents. They can sense when you are thinking they are awful parents. That is why it is so important to think positive thoughts about them as you greet them. The more they can sense that you care, the more receptive they will be to what you have to say.

Give Sincere Compliments

Most people like to hear nice things about themselves (Dawson, 1992). Many people hear all the things they do wrong rather than the things they do right. It's nice to hear nice things too. Get in the habit of giving sincere compliments to people. Do it with your family. Do it with your friends. Do it with your students, and do it with parents. Do it because you genuinely care, not to manipulate or persuade. This world would be a really wonderful place if everyone looked for good things in others. So when you see the parent, if there is something to compliment, do it. It opens the doors to communication.

Be Empathetic

Even though you have an issue you want to discuss with the parents, be empathetic (Dawson, 1992). Parents can sense if you really care about them and their children. When you are empathetic, you sense what the parent is feeling. For example, Mrs. Smith is a parent at your school. You have set up an appointment to meet with her to talk about her son Samuel's misbehavior. When she walks into the room, you immediately "read" her mood and sense that she is very sad. You look at her and say,

"Are you OK, Mrs. Smith?" She says, "I just found out that my favorite uncle passed away." You say to her, "I'm so sorry." You have been empathetic to her feelings, and you have just established rapport. Once rapport is established, it is easier for you to talk and for her to listen, and even better, a relationship of caring has been established.

Dress for Success

Dress professionally. Even though it may be inappropriate to judge others by appearances, when parents first get to know you, they often judge you by what they see.

Lift the Weight

When the situation gets heavy, it can literally weigh you down in negativity. Instead, keep it lighter. Before you meet with the parent, think of something that makes you happy. Picture in your mind something that makes you laugh. Think of a child that has said something that brought a smile to your face. Think of something a child said or did that made you giggle. It will help you lighten up and put things in perspective.

It is not always appropriate to think of something funny. For example, when you have to tell parents that you suspect their child has a serious problem that will affect that child's future, it is inappropriate to think of something funny; however, it is still important to keep yourself lighter prior to the meeting. If you are filled with dread at what you have to say, the parent will sense that. Do research ahead so you can offer the parent choices in how to handle the situation. Look for beacons of hope to impart to the parent. Mr. Carlson spoke with a parent with four children, two diagnosed with Autism Spectrum Disorder (ASD). That is a heavy load. She was feeling guilty because she was so busy taking her two children with ASD for their treatments that she could not spend as much time with her other two children. Mr. Carlson spoke to this mom with compassion and empathy as he told her about the misbehavior of one of her children. He kept it light and hopeful and, together, they came up with a plan of alternatives for this child. That's what you have to do too. Offer hope.

Walk, Stand, Sit, and Talk With Confidence

Your posture presents a picture of confidence or lack of confidence. Make sure your posture projects confidence. Practice standing straight (Decker, 1988). Stand in front of a wall with your head, neck, shoulders, and heels touching the wall. Slowly walk away from the wall keeping your body erect. Do this several times a day until it becomes a habit for you to stand and walk tall. When you have erect posture, it will help you sit straighter and talk with more confidence.

Avoid the "I'm Right" Game

When you speak to parents, be careful to not get into the game of who is right and who is wrong (Gill, 1999). There are no winners in that game, because when one person seems to win, the other person loses. And once that parent has lost, the game is over. Have you ever watched a legal battle being fought in a courtroom on television? The two sides each think they are right. They present argument upon argument. They put each other down as they speak about why their side is right and the other side is wrong. At the end of the trial, a jury determines one side as the winner. The two sides do not reach across the aisle and say, "Great, we can be a team now." Instead, they often leave thinking how they can appeal the verdict. It is the same with arguing to see who is right and who is wrong. There will be no winners. There will be appeals that can go on for a long time. The child who is in the middle loses this battle. That is the ultimate loser, and you and the parents also lose because you have lost an opportunity to work together to help the child.

Do not allow yourself to react. Do not become:

- Flustered
- Angry
- Frustrated
- Upset
- Sidetracked

Stay calm and collected. Stay focused on what you need to convey. Remember, your words make a difference. What you say can help or hinder your students. The calmer you are, and the more hope you offer, the more you increase the chance of working together as a team with parents on behalf of their children.

PRACTICE MAKES PERFECT

When I started Chapter 5, the chapter on listening skills, I said that communication is an art. An artist may have all of the things needed, but that artist will not be able to make a beautiful painting without lots of practice. It is the same with listening skills and assertive skills. In this chapter you have learned many powerful strategies that are extremely effective in getting others to listen to what you have to say. Just like the artist needs to practice to have it right, so too will you need to practice. Practice defining the problem. Write the problem down. Then write out a power request. Once you have that written, practice saying it. Do it until you feel you have it mastered. Do the same with the other strategies in this chapter. Practice the other elements of power persuasion. Have posture that reflects confidence and poise. Some of these may come more naturally, and others may involve more practice. The more you practice, the better you will get. Practice does make perfect.

Parent Conferences **7**

An Ounce of Prevention That Prevents a Pound of Problems

Conferences can be viewed as an ounce of prevention that prevents a pound of problems.

—Marlyn Appelbaum

Conferences are an excellent way to begin a partnership with parents to ensure that conflicts do not later arise. Here is a story that helps to illustrate the importance of fostering each unique teacher–parent relationship.

When two people get married, they do not generally get to choose their in-laws. Instead, they choose each other. When you begin teaching each school year, you receive "your" students. They are your students for better or for worse throughout the school year. You are "married" to them. Just as spouses do not get to choose their in-laws, you too do not get to choose your new "in-laws," the parents of your students. To be most successful with your students, you too have to establish a warm and caring relationship with your "in-laws." They are part of the marriage too, for better or for worse, for the entire school year. It is your job to ensure that it is for better, and not for worse. When it is worse, there will be hard-to-handle situations and hard-to-handle people.

Conferences are opportunities to build partnerships and foster communication. The conference is the first real time set aside to get to know each other. Even though you may have met the parent before, it was probably a quicker meeting. It's like the first time that married couples get to spend time with their in-laws. Everyone is looking each other over, hoping for the best, and feeling a little nervous. Conferences can be viewed as an ounce of prevention that prevents a pound of problems.

SET THE SCENE: THE FOCUS FACTOR

Set up your classroom so that it is a warm and welcoming place. Also, keep in mind the "focus factor." In order for both you and the family members to communicate, create a room that is calm and relaxing. You may want to have calming music playing in the background. Add some natural lighting to "warm up" the room. You can do this by adding a floor or table lamp. The calmer your room, the more parents and you will be able to focus on what is being said.

Have Comfortable Seating

Make sure the seating is comfortable for both you and the parent (Jordan, Reyes-Blanes, Peel, Peel, & Lane, 1998). Have the parent sit across from you at a table or sit side by side. Make sure that the chairs are the same height. If you tower over parents, there are some parents who might be immediately on guard rather than comfortable. Avoid student desks and seats. They are often not as comfortable because they are so small. It can be quite embarrassing for a parent who has a large frame to have to sit in a tiny chair that feels like it may break at any moment. That is not a good way to foster a parent partnership.

Dress for Success

Wear clothing that is attractive, conservative, and professional. Mrs. Landon attended a conference at her son Kyle's school. His teacher, Miss Staffield, had on a T-shirt, casual pants, and sandals. Her hair was unkempt and her T-shirt was stained. The slacks were frayed at the cuffs with big threads hanging out over sandals. Her socks looked like they once were white but were now grayish. Miss Staffield walked over to a table to get some papers for the conference slouching as she walked as though she did not have a care in the world. They sat down at a table to talk, and Mrs. Landon noticed Miss. Staffield had a big earring on her tongue. Mrs. Landon tried to listen to what Miss Staffield was saying to her about her son, but she kept staring at the tongue earring and thinking about this teacher's total appearance.

It is important to remember when preparing for a conference that there are people who do judge people by how they look. Think carefully about what you will wear. Take extra time with your appearance. Dress for success. The success will be becoming a team with parents of your students.

Be Prepared

Get lots of rest ahead of time so that you are alert and prepared for anything. You never know what questions or statements you will hear. Mr. Jacobs was a teacher having his first conference of the school year with Mr. and Mrs. Bender. Mr. Jacobs told them that their son had a problem with misbehavior. He said that it was interfering with their son's learning and that the youth had a hard time paying attention. Mrs. Bender kept looking off into space as Mr. Jacobs spoke. Her husband said, "He probably takes after my wife. She is schizophrenic and sometimes hears voices." And then, Mr. Bender leaned forward and said, "There's more. We think our son is evil and has come into the world to do bad things to others." Mr. Jacobs sat there nodding his head as he listened. Mr. Bender went on to say his father had killed himself. He said that sometimes he felt like doing this. While Mr. Bender listened, he tried not to show any reaction. That was a new one for him! He did know that he had to win those parents over or they would continue to believe their son was bad or evil. Their son had a problem paying attention at times, and he could be mischievous, but Mr. Bender did not believe that he was evil. He resolved to get them to work with him as a team. While his parents may still have had preconceived beliefs about their son, their son did do well in Mr. Bender's class. His parents became more and more cooperative as the school year progressed.

Send Family Profile Sheets Home

Some students live with their parents, and others live in other arrangements. It's important for you to know who is coming to the conference and that person's relationship to the student. Sometimes a teacher has assumed that an older parent was a grandparent. Nowadays there are all types of families, and you need to be prepared. You also need to know the surname of the parent or guardian who is coming to the conference. Do not assume that it is the same as the child's name.

A great way to do this is to send family profile sheets home with students (Mariconda, 2003; (see Figure 7.1). Students interview their parents and complete the information on the sheets. They bring the sheets back to school. The sheets contain names of family members as well as other pertinent data. A fun thing to do is to have students bring in a photo of the person coming to the conference or draw a picture of the person. This becomes part of the student portfolios, and parents enjoy seeing their own photos or the drawings their children made representing them.

Figure 7.1

The Family Profile

Student's name _____

Family member's name _____

Relationship to student _____

Favorites

Color_____

Animal _____

Book _____

Food _____

Hobby _____

Subject in school _____

Restaurant _____

Who were your "heroes" when you were growing up? _____

_____

_____

_____

What is your favorite motto or saying? _____

_____

_____

_____

We are looking forward to meeting you at the parent–teacher conference.

THE CONFERENCE

Because conferences are so important, you need to be completely prepared (Jordan et al., 1998). They can make or break your relationship with families and this in turn, can make or break your relationship with students.

Carefully Plan Important Issues

Plan ahead what you hope to accomplish (Mariconda, 2003). Decide what information you need to discuss with the parent. You may have a long list. Choose only two or three of the most important concerns to be addressed. It is important not to overwhelm the parent.

Check Your Negatives at the Door

If you have strong negative feelings about the student, make sure that you cool off before you meet the parent. It is important that you are objective when you meet with the parent. Parents can sense when you are negative about them or their children.

Role-Play Ahead of Time

If you do have students who are more difficult and you are concerned about the conference and how to say the right thing to parents, role-play the situation ahead of time (Million, 2005). You can do this with another teacher or even with the principal or assistant principal if it's a really important conference. If you do role-play with another person, be sure it is one who can keep confidentiality. You can also role-play in front of a mirror. The more you practice the words you want to say, the easier it will be the day you actually meet.

Use the Behavior Notebook

If the student has a behavior problem, be sure to have the behavior notebook previously discussed in Chapter 4. The misbehaviors are listed and signed by the student. This is concrete evidence that clearly demonstrates to a parent that there is a problem. It is hard to argue with a child's writing and signature documenting the problem.

Accommodate Parent Times Whenever Possible

When sending home notes for the conference, strive to accommodate the parent's schedule whenever possible (Stevens & Tollafield,

2003). It will help gain cooperation and show parents that you care. Most parents work. Some can take time off from work and others cannot. Keep this in mind when setting up schedules. There are some caring parents who may cancel several times because of crises at work that are beyond their control. Stay patient and reschedule. Ask them to give you several times of day that work best for them, and then try to find the time that works best for you so that it is a mutually agreed upon time.

Even the most well-intentioned parent can miss a conference. Their schedules are often jam-packed. Send a reminder of the time, date, and place to the parent again a couple of days before the conference.

Include directions on how to find your classroom and where to park. Wandering through schools can be like wandering through a maze if you do not know where to go. Parents may get frustrated before they ever arrive in your classroom because they were lost within the school. This is something you do not want to happen. When you provide clear directions on how to find your classroom and where to park, you can help prevent problems before they happen. Make sure to have your name on the door so that it easier to locate your room once parents are in the correct corridor.

Have a Comfy Waiting Area

Sometimes parents come earlier than they anticipated to the conference. Set up several chairs in the hallway outside your door. Have a sign indicating that you will be with them soon. If it's possible, have some cookies, crackers, or pretzels for a snack with a little sign saying, "Welcome. Feel free to have a snack. I'll be with you soon."

Include a bin with a sampling of student textbooks for parents to view while they are waiting for you to begin. When they do come into the classroom, be sure to apologize for any inconvenience that a wait may have caused.

Do Not Disturb

Arrange for no interruptions during a conference. It is disturbing to be interrupted at a crucial moment. Privacy is a big issue for parents. They may start talking about their child and totally stop when someone walks into the room. This needs to be a time in which you are not disturbed. Add a "Do Not Disturb" sign outside the door to your classroom while you are meeting with parents.

Have a Welcoming Classroom

Make your classroom parent friendly. Have student work on display. Include every student in your class. Parents generally will look around the classroom to find their children's work. Have "welcome parent" signs up in several places and in several languages as discussed in Chapter 1. Have the students make the signs. Involve the students in ideas for what the signs should say and how they should be decorated. Some students will tell their parents about the welcome signs before the parents come. This opens the doors to having your classroom be a warm and friendly place.

Welcome Parents

The best decoration is your own smile as you welcome parents. My own personal experience with my two children is a living testimony to this. My daughter was several years older than my son and started school before he did. When I went to her parent–teacher conferences I always heard comments such as, "She is a delight to have in class," and "Wish we had more like her." When my son started kindergarten, I was excited to meet his teacher. I was assigned times for the two conferences. My daughter's conference was first. I went in and met her teacher and saw some of her work and heard over and over again, "She is a delight to have in my classroom." I proudly left that room feeling wonderful. I walked down a flight of stairs to the kindergarten classrooms. I had on a big name tag that said, "Maryln Appelbaum." I walked into the kindergarten classroom and saw the teacher was speaking to another parent. I walked over near them so she could notice my name and know that I was Marty's mother. I could see that she noticed my name tag, but she avoided eye contact. When she was through speaking to the other parent, I walked over to her and proudly said, "Hi, I'm Maryln Appelbaum, Marty's mom." She gave me a withering look and sarcastically said, "Yes, I know." I felt devastated. Before she could even say another word to me, I too felt like I knew two things about this teacher! The first was that I hated her! I felt humiliated. The second thing I knew beyond a shadow of a doubt was that I was not going to like anything she said, and if she could be that rude, that it was probably all lies anyhow. That was the power of the lack of a warm greeting! It later turned out that my son misbehaved whenever he had close work because he had a vision problem and could not see the work. But by then it was too late. My first impression was the lasting impression. And it is the same with the first impressions of all your parents, so take time to sincerely greet them warmly. It makes anything you have to say more palatable.

Greet parents warmly (Jordan et al., 1998). Shake hands and introduce yourself, "Hi, I'm Pat McMartin, Troy's teacher, and I'm really glad to meet you, Mrs. Clay." Try to appear unhurried even if you ran a bit late. All parents want to feel that you are not going to rush through what you have to say. They want to feel important and that their child is important to you. Do set time limits when you welcome them so that they know that there will be an ending time.

Have a Work Portfolio

Work portfolios are excellent concrete ways to show parents exactly what their children are doing (Wilford, 2004). This is effective for both elementary and secondary students. Have one for each student. Involve the students in choosing the work to be placed in the portfolio. Include a note from the student to the parent in the portfolio. Have students write individualized notes to their parents. Almost all parents smile when they see the unique handwriting of their children addressed to them.

Include a blank page in the portfolio for parents to return a positive note to their children. When children come back into the classroom, they will see that their parents did attend the conference and their parents' letters. Make sure to tell parents to keep the letters to their children upbeat and positive.

Use Systematic Observations

Prepare for the conference by planning time to observe each student (Wilford, 2004). Observe students during different times of day to see how they behave during varying times. You may discover that different conditions produce different types of behaviors and learning.

Mrs. Thompkins was concerned about Stephanie's erratic behavior and learning. She decided to do some observations to get a fuller picture of how Stephanie functioned. She did this while teaching other students. She carried a little notebook in her pocket and wrote down the times of day and the varying behaviors. She discovered that Stephanie was easily distracted and then had problems focusing. She kept her notes as part of a file so that she could give more specific examples of Stephanie's behavior at the conference with Stephanie's family (see Figure 7.2).

Figure 7.2

Example of Systematic Observation

Stephanie W., October 3rd

9:00 Concentrates on seat work

9:01 Looks around room

9:02 Gets up and walks to pencil sharpener

9:03 Sits back down and looks around

KEY POINTS TO ENHANCE CONFERENCES

Listen, listen, and listen some more. Find out how the parent is thinking and feeling about the student. It will help you understand the student's behavior. Use the skills you have learned in this book. Sometimes, students are doing fine in school, yet parents may have other worries about their children. Everything that happens in children's lives generally has an effect on how children react when they come to school. If the parent is worried about the child's behavior, follow through and find out why the parent is worried.

Kathy Jorgens was Kiley's teacher. Kiley was a quiet child who studied hard and got good grades. When Kathy Jorgans met with Kiley's parents, she was surprised to learn that they were very concerned about Kiley's eating habits. They suspected that she might have an eating disorder. She listened to their fears and then made some suggestions for them to get help for Kiley.

Be careful to not be judgmental. Do not to criticize parents either directly or indirectly. They will become offended and shut down. It doesn't have to be your words. It can be the looks you give them that reflect your criticism or blame.

Do not get ahead of parents. Just like children may process information more slowly or more rapidly, so, too, do parents. Check for understanding before going on to new points. You can do this by saying, "So now that we have found a solution for _____, how about if we move on to _____." This opens the door for the parent who is processing the information more slowly, to tell you that he or she still has something to address. Some parents may be repetitive about the information wanting to stay focused on just one thing when you want to move on. If that is the case, and you feel very sure that the parent understands, say, "If it's OK with you, I would like to move on to the next topic. I'm worried we will run out of time and not be able to cover everything. If you want, we can make a new appointment to meet again."

Stay calm and focused throughout the conference. Your attitude is contagious. When you are calm, it will help the parent to also be calm.

Stay aware of the parent's facial expressions, gestures, and voice. These all will provide you with clues to the parent's emotions. Mr. Smith, William's father, said that he totally understood about William's misbehavior. He smiled as he listened. But Mrs. Cordan, William's teacher noticed that Mr. Smith's arms were crossed across his chest and his facial expression was one of anger even as he smiled.

THE FIVE-STEP APPROACH
TO TELLING PARENTS NEGATIVE NEWS

1. Establish a Connection

Start the conference by telling parents something positive about their child (Million, 2005). That is a must. Saying something positive serves several functions. First, it lets them know that you care. Parents don't care how much you know until they know how much you care. Second, it tells them that you really know their child. They know that their child is just one of many students. When they hear something positive that they know is true, it tells them that you have taken time to get to know their child. Third, when you tell them something positive that they know to be true about their child, they typically nod their heads to indicate "yes" in agreement with you. It starts the conference on a positive note of agreement rather than disagreement.

Jenny Brody was Zachery's teacher. He was a difficult student constantly challenging her authority as a teacher. When she met with Zachery's parents, she started off the conference by telling them that Zachery really enjoyed P.E. and that he was really good at it. His dad nodded his head, "yes," and then said, "Zachery has always loved sports." You too need to find something positive to say about each student and get parents to nod their heads "yes." This starts the conference out with the parents agreeing with you.

2. Establish Yourself as Knowledgeable

It is important that parents respect you so that they will listen to the things you tell them. This is especially true when you are going to tell them something negative about their children. An excellent way to do this is to tell them something you do with their children that "works." It may be the only thing you do that works, but it does work. When parents hear that you have something that you do that works, they often look at you with new respect. Many parents do not like to admit that they have problems in the home with their children when they are confronted with misbehavior. They may even say things like, "My child never does that at home." However, they still want to know that there is someone who does know how to manage their children in a positive manner that is effective.

3. Ask for Parent Involvement

Children's parents want to be seen as colleagues (Stevens & Tollafield, 2003). They want to be involved. The truth is that they share a common goal with you, and that is to improve their children's learning and behavior—to prepare their child for the future.

Ask them questions like these:

"How do you think we should handle this?"

"Do you have any ideas?"

"What works for you at home?"

When you ask parents for their input, it opens the doors to cooperation. Two-way communication is a must (Haviland, 2003). Parents need to feel that they have a voice. When parents give their input, they know that their viewpoints are encouraged and respected. It opens the doors to teamwork so that you and the parents can work together on behalf of their children.

4. Come Up With Solutions

Brainstorm solutions. Write them down. Together, choose the best and come up with a plan. Think through the plan to ensure that it is something that will be effective (Stevens & Tollafield, 2003). Write the plan down. Include all the resources you and parents will need. You may want to recommend a specific book for parents to use at home. Jessie's teacher recommended that his parents read a book that had helped her with classroom management. She wanted the parents to read the book so that they could use some of the same strategies.

Some of the resources may be people. Together, you may decide that it would be good for the student to see the school counselor. You may even decide that the child needs to see a physician. You could decide that the child needs a peer with whom to study.

5. Follow Through

A plan is only as good as the follow-through. End the conference with a plan to follow through and methods to communicate to determine progress. You may pass daily notes, use e-mail, or meet again in a month to talk about progress.

When the conference is ended, it is a good idea to give the parents a form documenting everything that was discussed (see Figure 7.3).

A week later, send home another conference follow-up that reviews in more detail the issues discussed and the action plan. It helps serve as a reminder to parents. It is amazing how soon some parents can forget. They get busy with their lives. When they receive the conference follow-up, it is a reminder that there is a plan and that they have a part in the plan (see Figure 7.4).

Figure 7.3

Conference Documentation

Student's name _____

Date of conference _____

Name of individual who attended conference _____

Relationship to student _____

Issues discussed _____

_____

_____

_____

_____

_____

_____

_____

_____

_____

_____

Action plan _____

_____

_____

_____

_____

_____

_____

_____

_____

_____

Teacher's signature _____

_____ _____, 20_____

Figure 7.4

Follow-Up for Conference

Dear _____,

Thank you so much for attending the conference concerning

_____held on _____ _____, 20_____.

It was great to meet and speak with you. I am looking forward to working with you as a team for your child.

As a positive reminder for both of us, I am outlining the suggestions and plans we made at the conference.

_____

_____

_____

_____

_____

_____

_____

_____

_____

_____

_____

_____

_____

_____

Thanks again for coming. It was a pleasure meeting you. I look forward to working together with you.

Sincerely yours,

_____

_____ _____, 20_____

CHECKLIST

Many people have a grocery list when they go shopping. They do this so that they will not forget anything important. Do this for conferences so that you too will remember everything that is important (see Figure 7.5).

Figure 7.5

Checklist for Parent Conferences

Before the Conference

- ❏ Did you plan for the conference and know what you would discuss?
- ❏ Did you try to accommodate parent times for the conference?
- ❏ Did you "cool down" any negative feelings?
- ❏ Did you do systematic observation of students?
- ❏ Did you send home family profile sheets?
- ❏ Did you arrange an area outside your classroom for the parent to wait?
- ❏ Did you have a snack in the waiting area?
- ❏ Did you decorate the room so that it is neat and attractive?
- ❏ Did you arrange comfortable seating for the conference?
- ❏ Did you prepare student portfolios?
- ❏ Did you treat the parent like a VIP?

During the Conference

- ❏ Did you help the parent to feel welcome?
- ❏ Did you tell the parent something positive about the child?
- ❏ Did you tell the parent something you do that works?
- ❏ Did you involve the parent in coming up with solutions?
- ❏ Did you encourage the parent to participate in the conference?
- ❏ Did your comments indicate interest and respect for the student?
- ❏ Did you both come up with an action plan for the child?
- ❏ Did you brainstorm solutions?
- ❏ Did you plan for following up the conference?
- ❏ Did you give the parent a conference documentation form?
- ❏ Did you close the conference on a positive note?
- ❏ Did you use power listening?
- ❏ Did you use power persuasion when and if it was needed?

Follow-Up

- ❏ Did you follow-up your conference with a notation of what was covered and suggestions made?

Parents as Partners **8**

*Enhancing Collaboration
and Teamwork*

*Each contact with a parent is an opportunity to become a team to
support the child.*

—Maryln Appelbaum

While each chapter in this book has been extremely important, in some ways, this one is the most important. It is most important because the other chapters gave you skills to get parents to come to the school, specific skills you need to communicate with parents, and specific skills for when there are problems, but this one gives you the skills you need to keep relationships going strong. The stronger the partnership you have with parents, the more you can get them involved. The more parents are actively involved in their children's education, the better students perform (Callison, 2004). Student achievement is affected, and so are student test scores (Moe, 2001). When there is a partnership of involvement with parents, schools benefit, parents benefit, and even better, the students benefit. The better the partnership, the fewer hard-to-handle parents you will have.

FORMING THE PARTNERSHIP:
A COLLABORATIVE RELATIONSHIP

Collaboration occurs when two or more people work together for the same goal. It involves trust, that each person will do their part (Adams & Christenson, 2000). This is not achieved overnight. It takes careful planning and communication using the strategies you have been learning in this book. The goal must always be teamwork to benefit the student (see Figure 8.1).

Figure 8.1

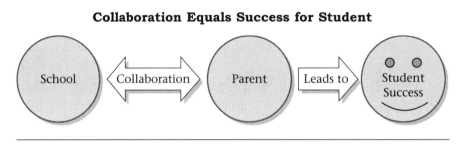

Collaboration Equals Success for Student

You can achieve collaboration. It begins with creating many opportunities for parental contact (Winn Tutwiler, 2005). The parents are the critical link that promotes student success. This chapter has many strategies to help you establish parents as partners.

Learn Student Interests

Parents of both elementary and secondary students like to know that you care about their children. Have elementary parents fill out a student interest survey at the beginning of the school year (Mendler, 2006). This works in two ways. First, it shows them that you are interested in their children, that you care, and that you want and value their comments. Second, it gives you great feedback so that you can work better with students. See Figure 8.2 for a student interest survey. Ensure that you have any communication to the parent translated into the parent's native language if you know or suspect the parent cannot read English.

You can use the same survey in secondary school although most students would prefer to complete their own survey. See Figures 8.3 for a survey for secondary students. Have students complete the survey so that you can learn more about them. The more you know about them, the better you will be able to build a relationship. The better the relationship you have with them, the happier students and parents will be. When you do meet with parents, they will sense that you know their children, and this will enhance collaboration.

The Red Notebook and the Colored Folder

You need an effective way to have continual communication with parents. When you send notes home to parents, they frequently are forgotten or lost. Parents also send notes that you may never receive. Here is a way to solve this problem. Have a red notebook for elementary students. It is a great way to improve two-way communication between the home and school (Epstein et al., 2002). Students each receive a bright

Figure 8.2

Student Interest Survey (Elementary School)

Dear Parent or Guardian,

I am looking forward to teaching your child this year and to getting to know you too. Your feedback is important to me. Please take a few minutes now and complete this survey so I can know more about your child. Together, we will make this a successful school year.

My child's name is _____

My child enjoys spending free time _____

_____

_____

_____

My child's favorite hobby is _____

My child's favorite subject in school is _____

Something that may affect my child's schoolwork is _____

_____

_____

_____

My child does not like _____

_____

_____

_____

I worry most about my child _____

_____

_____

_____

I would like your help with my child _____

_____

_____

_____

My goal for my child this school year is _____

_____

_____

_____

Parent or Guardian's signature _____

_____ _____, 20_____

Figure 8.3

Student Interest Survey (Secondary School)

Student's name _____

I enjoy spending free time _____

_____

_____

_____

_____

_____

My favorite subject in school is _____

My favorite famous person is _____

My least favorite subject in school is _____

My goal for this term is _____

_____

_____

_____

_____

_____

I would like help with _____

_____

_____

_____

_____

_____

Student's signature _____

_____ _____, 20_____

---

red notebook. When you have something to share with a parent, write it in the notebook. Parents answer you back in the notebook. It's difficult for students to lose a notebook that stands out so easily. There is a DVD rental company that sends out DVDs to their customers using bright red wrappings. My friends who are subscribers tell me that they have never lost one of the DVDs. They stand out among all their other mail because of the bright red wrapping. So too will the bright red notebook stand out for you, parents, and students.

Use this same concept with secondary students. Instead of a bright red notebook, which is large and can be embarrassing for students, have a colored transparent folder. It easily will fit into student notebooks and backpacks and can be transported home and back to school easily.

Include Parents in Student Learning

The more that parents are included in their children's learning, the better students learn (Davis, 2000). Students get higher grades, have better attendance, do their homework more consistently, and develop positive attitudes toward school and to homework. More important, students develop more self-confidence in learning and have more positive attitudes toward school.

Reading Togetherness

Have a parent night that teaches parents the art of reading together with their children (Powell-Smith, Stoner, Shinn, & Good, 2000). Have some interesting books. You or a storyteller can demonstrate how to read a short portion of a book to capture the interest of the students. Here are some tips to include.

- Be enthusiastic
- Change your voice tone so it gets louder and softer
- Be dramatic
- Ask fun questions
- Introduce the book in a fun way so that students want to hear it
- Invite students to summarize key points at different points in the story

Secondary students also can have reading togetherness. Have a special article in a student textbook that students can read and then get the opinions of their parents on it. It's fun to get something controversial. You can also use current events in newspapers and have the parents and their children share their opinions on the reading.

Book of the Month

Every month recommend a special book for family members. Write a short review of the book and describe how it will benefit parents. At my own private school, I recommended a book on parent-child communication. I ordered them and had them available for resale for parents. It was a small fund raiser, but even better, it helped parents learn to be on the same page with the school by providing them with tools for effective discipline and communication with their children.

Reading Journals

Reading journals is another way to have parents and their children read together (Allen, 2007). Students choose books to read at home with their parents. They take turns reading to each other. When they are finished reading, it's time to write in the journal. Students may write down their responses to the reading, or they can dictate their responses to parents for them to write. Parents may choose to write their responses too. This can be done for any subject that involves reading. It is a way of transforming an ordinary reading of material into something more fun for families. It's a great way to get parents involved in what their children are learning.

Secondary students can do this too. Instead of taking turns reading pages in a book, they can simply read and write in their journals. Parents can read the same pages and add their own comments. This has an additional benefit of increasing parent-child communication.

Parent Interviews

This is a wonderful strategy that works on all grade levels. Students interview their parents about a subject they are studying in school. Parents can tell their memories of having taken this subject or about their hopes for their children as a result of having learned the subject. It's open-ended. The important thing is that the whole family is involved in what students are learning.

Family Bios

Every family has a story about their heritage (Allen, 2007). Family members can draw their family trees or write a short history of their family. They may also use this as a tribute to one of their family members.

My Hero

When studying about different famous individuals, students can also choose to interview a family member who is "famous" in their eyes. They interview the person and then write the results of the interview.

Author Fairs

Have each student choose their favorite book and their favorite character in that book (Power, 1999). Students become authors "writing about their favorite characters." Depending on the age of students, students can even dress up as the characters. Parents come to school to meet the authors and get their autographs.

This can be modified for older students to choose a character in social studies or science or history. They can act out the characters in class, write brief papers on their characters, and then autograph the papers with both their signatures and what they think the signatures of the real authors would look like. Put these in student portfolios to share with parents when they come to school.

The Gathering Place

A parent gathering place is a special space for parents to gather and become more involved with the school (McAllister Swap, 1993). Have a parent gathering place that is a cozy comfortable room where parents can come to connect with other parents, volunteer, or obtain resources. Parents work on class projects in the gathering place, check out material from a parent library, meet with teachers, or just drop in for a cup of coffee to relax and meet other parents. There are pamphlets, books, DVDs, and family games that parents can check out for use at home.

Have teacher bins in the gathering place. Each bin has work that needs to be done. It can be cutting, coping, or laminating with instructions on what needs to be done. The instructions are in English and may also be in a second and even third language that applies to the parents in your school. Parents go into the room when they have free time, choose a bin with work, and do it. They talk to other parents as they work. Teachers drop in during their breaks. It becomes like a "family room" at home filled with quiet conversation.

Decorate the room with posters with positive sayings. Parents and students can make some of the posters. Make sure the sayings are translated into the languages that meet the needs of your school population. Add a few plants to warm up the room and even a couple of cozy rocking chairs in addition to regular tables and chairs. The goal is to make it a home away from home for parents so that they feel comfortable with the school, and part of the school.

"We Are Family"

Make school a fun place for parents to come. Have a fun family time (Morehand-Rose, 2008). Invite the entire family out for a day or evening of fun activities throughout the school. The goal is to develop a sense of community and get family support. Set up different classrooms as game rooms in which family members play Bingo, cards, and board games. Have other rooms for arts and crafts, make-and-takes, and even movies. Use the gym for sport tournaments and dance lessons. Have student work on display throughout the building. Have volunteer tables for parents to sign up to volunteer for school activities.

Moms and Muffins

Invite moms and special pals to a fun time with a special speaker. Serve muffins and invite moms to sign up to volunteer. Spice it up by having a fashion show every couple of months using local merchants to talk about and showcase the latest styles.

Dads and Doughnuts

Invite dads and special pals to come to school once a month. Serve doughnuts and bring in speakers about relevant topics for dads like business or sports and talk about how dads and special pals can become involved in the school.

Breakfast Meet and Greet

This is a great way for family members to meet other family members and the faculty. It can also be held evenings and called an "Evening Meet and Greet."

Monthly Coffee Hour

This is a time when parents gather to talk and give input as to how their children are doing and any other needs they may have.

Volunteer Appreciation

Appreciate the family members who volunteer. Send home thank-you notes. Have marquees with the names of all the volunteers who helped. Have volunteers sign in every time they come and sign out when they leave. Honor the individuals who have volunteered the most number of hours at a special luncheon. Hand out award certificates honoring all those who volunteer for their participation in helping the school.

Parenting Skill Workshops

An excellent way of creating parents as partners is to offer courses in parenting skills (McAllister Swap, 1993). Invite parents and teachers to sign up. You can bring in people to teach the course, or you can create your own course based on a book or DVD. It becomes a bonding experience as parents share their struggles and their experiences. You will also see a noticeable difference in the way the students behave as their parents implement the strategies.

Parenting Needs Workshops

Determine the needs of parents within your school and offer workshops to meet those needs (McAllister Swap, 1993). For example, if there is a high rate of unemployment in your area, you may offer a workshop on how to write résumés. Include workshops in which local merchants display and talk about their merchandise so that parents learn more about their neighborhoods' resources.

Having Fun

When parents do come to school, make sure they have fun. The more fun they have, the more they will want to come back. Play games that also give you more information about what parents want.

Poster Share

Have large poster-size sheets of paper posted around the room (Boult, 2006). Each sheet has a heading, and the rest of the sheet is blank. Parents walk around and fill in the sheets that apply to their children. Then they walk around and read the other sheets. Be sure to have a translator if needed. You get to find out more about them, and they get to find out more about other families too. I have done this and it creates a fun and bonding atmosphere. Here are some ideas for the poster share:

- *My child's favorite subject is . . .*
- *The number one thing I want for my child is . . .*
- *I would like the school to have more . . .*
- *The best way you could communicate with me is . . .*
- *I would come to school to hear more about this topic . . .*

It's a Dog's World

This is a fun game that creates laughter, teamwork, and a sense of camaraderie. Name aloud four different breeds of dogs. Each breed is represented by a different corner of the room. When parents hear the name of the dog they like best, they go to that corner of the room. The breeds I have used for this game are poodle, collie, beagle, and Chihuahua. It's a lot of fun to watch parents get into their "dog groups." Once the parents are in their groups, tell them to work together to choose a name for their dog that they will be sharing with the others in the room. Next, have them choose a favorite characteristic of their dog. Have each group take turns sharing with the others the name they chose and the favorite characteristic. This is a great way for parents to have fun, meet each other, and participate.

Use Classroom Strategies

Use some fun teaching strategies at your parent meetings. Introduce a topic that students will be learning or have already learned, or just introduce something fun. My favorite topic to get parents involved is the cup. I hold up a cup, and I have the parents do a series of activities about the cup.

Uses of Cup

The first activity is that the parents each write on their own sheet of paper as many ideas as they can think of for the use of the paper cup.

Do a Pair-Share

The parents each get a partner and share their ideas and get even more ideas to add to their list.

Use the Two-Four-Eight Strategy

The partners get another set of partners and share, so now there are four people. The four people share and then get another group of four people so now there are eight people (Boult, 2006). By now, they have developed a long list of uses for the paper cup.

Whole Audience Participation

The entire audience shares their uses of the paper cup to get even more ideas.

Purpose

When they are finished sharing, parents are told that this is a teaching strategy that is used with their children to get them enthused to learn about a subject.

Student Success Night

Have a special evening in which you tell parents how to help their students be successful in school. Include social, emotional, and learning skills. Homework is an important aspect of success. Teach parents how to coach their children to do their homework (Power, 1999). Give parents handouts for homework (see Figures 8.4 and 8.5).

The Homework Log

The homework log (see Figure 8.5) is an excellent way for students and their parents to keep track of their homework. The column labeled

Figure 8.4

Strategies for Homework

- Have a regularly scheduled time each day for children to do homework. Children do better when it is the same time every day. They develop a routine.
- Teach children to set a timer for doing homework. Begin with a shorter period of time and work up to a longer time. Schedule homework breaks for five minutes each time.
- Have a special place for doing homework. It needs to be a quiet place that is free of distractions including the sound of television, music, or phone.
- Have a special desk or table that is not used for anything other than homework.
- Ask to see the homework before it is finished.
- Make sure the child understands the directions.
- Check in if it seems to be taking a long time.
- Break the assignments into more manageable chunks if needed.
- Look at all homework when it is finished.
- Reinforce the child for completing homework. Some families offer a special family treat such as game time or a snack together when homework is completed.

Figure 8.5

Homework Log

Name _____ Week __ of _____

Subjects	Monday	Tuesday	Wednesday	Thursday	Friday

Teacher's signature _____

Note to parents: Please initial the homework in the appropriate column for the day once it is completed.

"subject" is the subject in which there is homework. There are six subject columns. Write in each subject column the name of the subject such as English and Math and Social Studies.

Under each day of the week, write the homework to be done for that subject. When students finish their homework, parents check to see if it is complete. If it is complete, the parent puts his or her initials in the box next to the homework.

HOW TO GET PARENTS TO FOLLOW THROUGH AT HOME

In some homes, the children are in charge rather than the parents. When these parents are asked to help their children follow through on assignments, they are already overwhelmed. They know that they cannot even follow through for something as simple as mealtime or bedtime let alone study time. Other parents may just be exhausted at the end of the day. Their goal is to just make it through another day of work, cooking, shopping, cleaning, and getting ready to do more of the same the next day. However, almost all parents want their children to succeed. They want them to be prepared to have good lives as adults.

Find out what parents want for their children. That is the key. If they want their children to succeed in school, you have a good chance of getting them to work with you as a team and to follow through for their children.

Once you know what they want, it is time to get them to commit to a plan for following through at home. "Mrs. Camu, do you agree that you want Javier to get better grades and pass his courses?"

Most parents will say, "Yes, I agree." Then it is time to come up with a simple plan. If it is too complex, it probably will not be followed. Talk about the red notebook or the colored transparent folder and how you will be passing it home and back so that you both can communicate. Then introduce the homework check sheet. Explain that this will be coming home each day with the student. The parent will always know the homework assignments for the week. Go over the steps in completing homework.

Help parents follow through by giving them a sample contract they can use at home. Contracts are effective with students (Knowles, 1986). They lead to self-directed learning. The contract is an individualized approach to ensure that students follow through at home. The parent gives the contract to the student, and they each sign the contract to show they are in agreement. The contract specifies what the student will do to fulfill the contract. Some parents promise that the student will receive something when the contract is fulfilled. The latter is not necessary. I have found that most students do what it says on the contract simply because it is written. See a sample contract in Figure 8.6.

Figure 8.6

Contract

I, _____,

will _____

_____

_____

_____

_____

_____

_____

_____

_____

_____

_____

_____

_____

_____

_____

_____

_____

_____

_____

_____

_____

_____

_____

_____

_____.

I will finish this by _____.

Student's signature _____

_____ _____, 20_____

Parent's signature _____

Stay in Contact

In Chapter 1, I said that e-mail was a good way to stay in contact. Most parents, depending on your school population, have e-mail. That is an easy way to stay in contact. A quick note to parents can go far toward establishing relationships (Mendler, 2006). I kept in touch with one of my grandchildren's teachers via e-mail. My grandson had some special needs following a long illness, and I was the one was in charge of his education. I developed relationships via e-mail with his teachers and his counselor. It was an awesome and quick way for me to find out how he was doing. You can do this too with your students and their parents. Send out a bright, colored note at the beginning of the school year to get the e-mail address of parent (see Figure 8.7).

Figure 8.7

Let's Stay in Touch

Hi,

I am your child's teacher this year. My name is _____.

I am looking forward to teaching your child this year. Here is a way that you can contact me. My e-mail address is _____

Please return this form with your e-mail address so I too can contact you. Together, we will ensure your child's success this year.

Child's name _____

Parent's name_____

Parent's e-mail address _____

Parent's daytime telephone number _____

CONCLUSION

As an educator, you have a very full schedule. There is a steady stream of paperwork that must be done as well as your work with students. Sometimes, it may seem like there aren't enough hours in the day to do all of your work and also establish partnerships with parents. But in the end, the time you take now, will save you time later. Every time that you use any of the skills that you have been learning in this book, you will be taking a step toward fostering teamwork and partnership and preventing hard-to-handle situations and parents.

I'm ending this book with a "parent's plea" that is a reminder of the importance of what you do—the importance of being partners. You make a difference. Your work lays the foundation for the future because the children are our future. And their future begins with working together with parents.

A PARENT'S PLEA TO TEACHERS

If you really want to get to know me, look inside. I may smile when deep inside, I'm worried. I may get angry when deep inside, I'm scared. I may be passive and rarely come to school, but I want you to know that my child means so much to me.

I have so many thoughts that race through my head: Will you like my child? Will you know my child, really know my child? Will you see the good qualities in my child? Will my child have friends? Will my child get good grades? Will my child be safe in your school? Will my child be influenced by peers and become someone I don't even recognize? Is my child smart? Can my child learn? Will my child be happy? Will my child have a bright future?

It's terrifying to think you are the one with the answers to all those questions. Not me! I am the one who brought this child into the world! Who are you to determine my child's future? Are you good enough? Can you really help my child?

Sometimes, I get so overwhelmed that I don't want to do anything. I don't want to come to school. I don't want to meet you. I act like I don't care. But deep inside, I do, I really do.

Other times, I get mad. I get mad that you are the one in control of my child's life. You are the one who determines if my child passes or fails. Not me!

Please help me. Help me by providing a safe haven for my child. Help me by being patient with me and with my child. Help me to see that you care, really care for my child. Help me to feel that I am not in this alone, that I have a partner in you. Help me, and you help my child. And together, we can make great things happen.

References

Adams, K., & Christenson, S. (2000). Trust and the family–school relationship: Examination of parent teacher differences in elementary grades. *Journal of School Psychology, 38*, 477–497.

Allen, J. B. (2007). *Creating welcoming schools: A practical guide to home–school partnerships with diverse families.* Newark, DE: Teacher College Press.

Appelbaum, M. (1995a). *How to listen so kids will talk.* Houston, TX: Appelbaum Training Institute.

Appelbaum, M. (1995b). *How to talk to kids so they will listen.* Houston, TX: Appelbaum Training Institute.

Appelbaum, M. (2009a). *How to handle hard-to-handle students.* Thousand Oaks, CA: Corwin.

Appelbaum, M. (2009b). *The one stop guide to implementing RTI: Academic and behavioral interventions, K–12.* Thousand Oaks, CA: Corwin.

Bender, Y. (2005). *The tactful teacher: Effective communication with parents, colleagues and administrators.* White River Junction, VT: Nomad Press.

Bergmann, S., Brough, J., & Shepard, D. (2008). *Teach my kid, I dare you! The educator's essential guide to parent involvement.* Larchmont, NY: Eye on Education.

Boult, B. (2006). *176 ways to involve parents: Practical strategies for partnering with families.* Thousand Oaks, CA: Corwin.

Bramson, R. M. (1981). *Coping with difficult people.* New York: Dell.

Brinkman, R., & Kirschner, R. (2002). *Dealing with people you can't stand: How to bring out the best in people at their worst.* New York: McGraw-Hill.

Callison, W. L. (2004). *Raising test scores: Using parent involvement.* Lanham, MD: Scarecrow Education.

Capek Tingley, S. (2006). *How to handle difficult parents: A teacher survival guide.* Fort Collins, CO: Cottonwood Press.

Davis, D. (2000). *Supporting parent, family, and community involvement in your school.* Portland, OR: Northwest Regional Educational Laboratory.

Dawson, R. (1992). *Secrets of power persuasion: Everything you'll ever need to get anything you'll ever want.* New York: Prentice Hall.

Decker, B. (1988). *The art of communicating: Achieving interpersonal impact in business.* Los Altos, CA: Crisp.

Drew, N. (2004). *The kids' guide to working out conflicts: How to keep cool, stay safe, and get along.* Minneapolis, MN: Free Spirit.

Epstein, J. L., Sanders, M. G., Simon, B. S., Clark Salinas, K., Rodriguez Jansorn, N., & Van Voorhis, F. L. (2002). *School, family, and community partnerships: Your handbook for action* (2nd ed.). Thousand Oaks, CA: Corwin.

Franzoi, S. L. (2000). *Social psychology* (2nd ed.). Boston: McGraw-Hill.

Gibbs, N. (2005). Parents behaving badly. *Time Magazine, 165*(3), 42–49.

Gill, L. (1999). *How to work with just about anyone: A 3-step solution for getting difficult people to change.* New York: Fireside Books.

Gordon, T. (2000). *Parent effectiveness training: The proven program for raising responsible children.* New York: Three Rivers Press.

Haviland, J. (2003). When parent group meetings please parents. *Education Digest, 68*(7), 51–56.

Henderson, A. T., Mapp, K. L., Johnson, V. R., & Davies, D. (2007). *Beyond the bake sale: The essential guide to family–school partnerships.* New York: New Press.

Hoover, E. (2008). Surveys of students challenge helicopter parent stereotypes. *Chronicle of Higher Education, 54*(21), ERIC, EJ786617.

Houston, M. B., & Bettencourt, L. A. (1999). But that's not fair! An exploratory study of student perceptions of student fairness. *Journal of Marketing Education, 21*(2), 84–97.

Jaksec, C. M., III. (2003). *The confrontational parent: A practical guide for school leaders.* Larchmont, NY: Eye on Education.

Jordan, L., Reyes-Blanes, M. E., Peel, B., Peel, H. A., & Lane, H. B. (1998). Developing teacher–parent partnerships across culture: Effective parent conferences. *Intervention in School & Clinic, 33*(3), 141–148.

Knowles, M. S. (1986). *Using learning contracts.* San Francisco: Jossey-Bass.

Kosmoski, G. J., & Pollack, D. R. (2000). *Managing difficult, frustrating, and hostile conversations: Strategies for savvy administrators.* Thousand Oaks, CA: Corwin.

Lasky, S. (2000). The cultural and emotional politics of teacher–parent interactions. *Teacher and Teacher Education, 16,* 843–860.

Lee, S. M., Kushner, J., & Cho, S. H. (2007). Effects of parent's gender, child's gender, and parental involvement on academic achievement of adolescents in single parent families. *Sex Roles, 56*(3/4), 149–157.

Mariconda, B. (2003). *Easy and effective ways to communicate with parents: Practical techniques and tips for parent conferences, open houses, notes home, and more that work for every situation.* New York: Scholastic Professional Books.

McAllister Swap, S. (1993). *Developing home–school partnerships: From concepts to practice.* New York: Teacher College Press.

McEwan, E. K. (2005). *How to deal with parents who are angry, troubled, afraid, or just plain crazy* (2nd ed.). Thousand Oaks, CA: Corwin.

McNaughton, D., Hamlin, D., McCarthy, J., Head-Reeves, D., & Schreiner, M. (2007). Learning to listen: Teaching an active listening strategy to preservice education professionals. *Topics in Early Childhood Special Education, 27*(4), 223–231.

Mendler, A. N. (2006). *Handling difficult parents: Successful strategies for educators.* Rochester, NY: Discipline Associates.

Million, J. (2005). Getting teachers set for parent conferences. *Education Digest, 70*(8), 56–56.

Moe, T. M. (2001). *A primer on America's schools.* Stanford, CA: Stanford University, Hoover Institution Press.

Morehand-Rose, R. (2008). *Appelbaum Training Institute teacher appreciation contest.* Sugar Land, TX: Appelbaum Training Institute.

Personality disorders: Sources of evidence. (1995). *Harvard Mental Health Letter, 95*(11), 6–8.

Politis, C. (2004). When a parent has inappropriate expectations. *Early Childhood Today, 18*(7), 8.

Powell-Smith, K. A., Stoner, G., Shinn, M. R., Good, R. H., III. (2000). Parent tutoring in reading using literature and curriculum materials: Impact on student reading achievement. *School Psychology Review, 29*(1), 5-23.

Power, B. (1999). *Parent power: Energizing home–school communication: Guide for teachers and schools.* Portsmouth, NH: Heinemann.

Rich, D. (1998). What parents want from teachers. *Educational Leadership, 55*(8), 37–39.

Rudney, G. L. (2005). *Every teacher's guide to working with parents.* Thousand Oaks, CA: Corwin.

Sanderson, B. E. (2005). *Talk it out: The educator's guide to difficult conversations.* Larchmont, NY: Eye on Education.

Smrekar, C., & Cohen-Vogel, L. (2001). The voices of parents: Rethinking the intersection of family and school. *Peabody Journal of Education, 76*(2), 75–100.

Stevens, B. A., & Tollafield, A. (2003). Creating comfortable and productive parent/teacher conferences. *Phi Delta Kappan, 84*(7), 521–525.

Umbreit, J., Ferro, J., Liaupsin, C. J., & Lane, K. L. (2007). *Functional behavioral assessment and function-based intervention: An effective, practical* approach. Upper Saddle River, NJ: Pearson Education.

Wherry, J. H. (2008). Working with difficult parents. *Principal, 87*(4), 12–12.

Whitaker, T., & Fiore, D. J. (2001). *Dealing with difficult parents and with parents in difficult situations.* Larchmont, NY: Eye on Education.

Wilford, S. (2004). Successful parent conferences. *Early Childhood Today, 18*(4), 12–14.

Winn Tutwiler, S. J. (2005). *Teachers as collaborative partners: Working with diverse families and communities.* Mahwah, NJ: Lawrence Erlbaum.

Yan, G. (2006). Why didn't they show up? Rethinking ESL parent involvement in K–12 education. *Canada Journal, 24*(1), 80–95.

Index

CORWIN

A SAGE Company

The Corwin logo—a raven striding across an open book—represents the union of courage and learning. Corwin is committed to improving education for all learners by publishing books and other professional development resources for those serving the field of PreK–12 education. By providing practical, hands-on materials, Corwin continues to carry out the promise of its motto: **"Helping Educators Do Their Work Better."**

Appelbaum
Training Institute

Appelbaum Training Institute (ATI) provides the latest, the best, and the most research-based information on the most current subjects in a fun and enjoyable manner through professional development, training, and resources to educators and parents of children of all ages and diverse backgrounds. The ATI motto is **"Building Bridges to the Future,"** and that is exactly what the Appelbaum Training Institute does every day in every way for educators across the world.